SIR JOHN MANDEVILLE

SIR JOHN MANDEVILLE
(à la barbe)
From a MS of Velser's translation in the
New York Public Library (Spencer Collection).

SIR JOHN
MANDEVILLE

The Man and his Book

BY

Henry Ikin

MALCOLM LETTS, F.S.A.

Benedick : 'I will fetch you a tooth-picker now from the furthest
inch of Asia; bring you the length of Prester John's foot; fetch
you a hair off the Great Cham's beard; do you any embassage to
the Pigmies.'

Much Ado about Nothing, Act II Scene I.

LONDON

THE BATCHWORTH PRESS

PUBLISHED IN 1949 BY
BATCHWORTH PRESS LTD.
20 TUDOR STREET, E.C.4

PR
2054
L4

PRINTED IN GREAT BRITAIN BY
JAMES UPTON LTD.
LONDON AND BIRMINGHAM

CONTENTS

CONTENTS

6

ILLUSTRATIONS

ILLUSTRATIONS

Preface

EXCEPT for Professor Hamelius' edition of the Cotton text, which was completed in 1923, there has been no serious work on Mandeville for nearly fifty years. Sir George Warner's monumental edition of the Egerton version was published in 1889 for the Roxburghe Club. A. W. Pollard's modernised Cotton text — a most scholarly piece of work — appeared in 1900. Dr. Pollard's edition is out of print and the Roxburghe Club books are expensive and difficult to obtain. There is a handy edition of Mandeville in the Everyman Series, but this is a reprint, with additions, of East's text of 1568, as reprinted by Ashton in 1887. What the English reader needs is a reprint of Wynkyn de Worde's or Pynson's edition, supplemented by the modernised Cotton text and by one or other of the abridged but independent and amusing versions in the Bodleian Library.[1] Then, and then only, will Mandeville come into his own. In the meantime, I hope this book will fill a gap and draw attention once more to one of the most delightful of all travel books, which has been somewhat neglected in recent years. That the author never visited the countries he describes, and that the book, as we have it, is a translation in which the author had no hand, makes no difference. As Dr. Pollard says in the introduction to his edition of the Cotton text, 'the book remains, and is none the less delightful for the mystery which attaches to it, and little less important in the history of English literature as a translation than as an original work. For, though a translation, it stands as the

---

[1] E. Museo, 116 and Rawlinson D. 99.

9

first, or almost the first, attempt to bring secular subjects within the domain of English prose, and that is enough to make it mark an epoch.' My debt to Sir George Warner is apparent throughout, and I desire to express my thanks to the President of the Roxburghe Club for permission to make use of this edition. Messrs. Macmillan & Co. Ltd. and Mrs. J. K. Roberts (Dr. Pollard's daughter) have kindly allowed me to quote freely from Dr. Pollard's version of the Cotton text. Nearly all my English quotations are from this version. No student of Mandeville can close his labours without acknowledging his debt to Mr. E. W. B. Nicholson, Dr. Vogels and Dr. Bovenschen, who, with Warner (between 1876 and 1891), laid the foundation for a new, approach to the whole Mandeville problem. It will probably never be solved, but I have re-stated the evidence, drawn my own conclusions, and tried to clear up several points. No examination of the German translations or the Brussels MS has been undertaken before. Some new light has been thrown on Outremeuse's connection with the book and, with the help of a valued collaborator, I have attempted a solution of the difficult problem of the alphabets. My thanks are also due to the officials of the British Museum, the Bodleian Library, the University Library, Cambridge, Chetham's Library, Manchester, the New York Public Library, the South African Public Library, Cape Town, the Bibliothèque Nationale, Paris, the Bibliothèque Royale, Brussels, and Leyden University for their courtesy in supplying photostats and answering enquiries, to Mr. Boies Penrose of Philadelphia for supplying photostats of an English MS, to Mr. Lionel Robinson, the well known bookseller, for allowing me to carry away and examine at leisure an important MS from the Castle Howard Library now in his possession, to my friend Mr. G. D. Painter for collaboration in one chapter and for his constant help and advice, and above all to my wife for much constructive criticism. I have revised and incorporated in my book a series of my notes which appeared in *Notes and Queries* between 1946 and 1948, and some paragraphs from an article on 'Lying Travellers' which appeared in the *Contempory Review* in July 1920. I am obliged to the editors of these journals for permission to do so. The picture map is the work of my niece, Miss Pamela B. Baldwin.

M.L.

BOOK ONE

The Man and his Times

*

CHAPTER I

The Man

'Sir John Mandevile . . . whose travayles in forraine regions and rare reportes are at this time admired through the world.'[1]

SIR JOHN MANDEVILLE tells us in the Prologue to his 'Travels' that he was a knight, albeit he was unworthy, that he was born in England in the town of St. Albans, and that he crossed the sea in 1322. He then continues: 'and hitherto [I] have been long time over the sea, and have seen and gone through many diverse lands, and many provinces and kingdoms and isles and have passed throughout Turkey, Armenia the little and the great; through Tartary, Persia, Syria, Arabia, Egypt the high and the low; through Lybia, Chaldea, and a great part of Ethiopia through Amazonia, Ind the less and the more, a great part; and throughout many other Isles that be about Ind; where dwell many diverse folks, and of diverse manners and laws, and of diverse shapes of men.' Except for the Epilogue, this is practically all he tells us about himself and any further details have to be gathered from other sources. It seems unkind to the memory of the man, whose name has been associated from our childhood with one of

[1] MS note by John Stow in Norden's *Descripion of Hertfordshire*, 1598, in the British Museum (Maps C. 7, b. 24).

13

the most delightful travel-books of all ages, to say that the author was an imaginary traveller, and that his book is a compilation, taken from the works of earlier writers, with additions gathered from every available book of reference, going back to Pliny, if not further. It has even been suggested that the book was not written by Mandeville at all, but by a Liége physician named Jean de Bourgogne who for some reason adopted the name of Mandeville. The note in the British Museum catalogue, which may well have been written by Sir George Warner, concludes as follows. 'It is probable that the name John de Mandeville should be regarded as a pseudonym, concealing the identity of Jean de Bourgogne, a physician at Liége, mentioned under the name of Joannes ad Barbam in the vulgate Latin version of the Travels,' and this is the line taken by other scholars, including Nicholson and Yule, in the article on Mandeville in the *Encyclopaedia Britannica*. I do not subscribe to this view. In my view it was Mandeville who wrote the book and it was Mandeville who took the name of de Bourgogne for reasons which I will give later. In other words, although the matter is by no means clear, the situation is reversed. Mandeville was de Bourgogne, not de Bourgogne Mandeville.

There are, however, still a number of loose threads. A mysterious personage now appears on the scene, one Jean d'Outremeuse (1338-1399), a notary of Liége, of whom little is known except that he compiled, among other works, a world-chronicle called *Myreur des Histors*, written in a French-Flemish dialect, which is difficult to read and on the whole extremely dull. Outremeuse tells us in Book IV (now lost) of the *Myreur*, how a modest old man known as Jean de Bourgogne, or Jean à la Barbe, confided on his death-bed to Outremeuse, in 1372, that his real name was John de Mandeville, who had fled from home in 1322 because he had slain a man of rank, and had bound himself therefore to traverse three parts of the world. The passage is worth quoting in full.

14

In the year 1372 there died in Liége on the 12th November a man
greatly distinguished by his birth who was content to be known by
the name of Jean de Bourgogne, called 'with the beard.' He opened
his heart however on his death-bed to Jean d'Outremeuse, his friend,
whom he appointed his testamentary executor. In truth he called
himself in the *précis* of his last will Master Jean de Mandeville,
Knight, Count of Montfort in England, lord of the isle of Campdi and
of Château Perouse. Having had the misfortune to kill, in his country,
a count whom he did not name, he obliged himself to traverse the
three parts of the world. Came to Liége in 1343. Although he was a
man of distinguished nobility he preferred to keep himself hidden.
For the rest, he was a great naturalist, a profound philosopher and
astrologer, to which he added in particular a singular knowledge of
medicine, rarely deceiving himself when expressing his opinion
concerning a patient, whether he would recover or not. Dying at
last, he was interred with the Guillelmin brothers in the suburb of
Avroy, as you will have been able to see more fully above.'[1]

We have here a definite statement that de Bourgogne
declared himself to be Mandeville, and the matter is carried
a step further and still further confused by a statement
in the Latin version of the 'Travels,' in which Mandeville
is made to say that when in Egypt he met a venerable
physician, whom he had known previously in Cairo, and
that long afterwards at Liége, on his way home, in 1355, he
recognised the same physician in Master John 'ad Barbam,'
and that Mandeville wrote his 'Travels' at his instigation
and with his help.

This appears, so far as is known, only in the Latin
vulgate edition of the 'Travels' (chap vii) and, as translated,
reads as follows.[2] After a description of the sultan's manner
of giving audience, the author is made to say:—

When I stayed at the court I saw about the sultan a venerable and
skilful physician sprung from our own parts. For he (the sultan) was
wont to keep about him physicians of diverse nations whose fame
had reached his ears. We met only rarely for conversation when my

[1] Warner, p. xxxiv Hamelius, II, p. 8. The extract from the lost fourth Book of
the *Myreur* was made by the Liége herald and genealogist Louis Abry (d. 1720),
from a copy of the *Myreur* made by Jean de Stavelot (d. 1449) who added a fifth
Book down to 1447. There seems no reason to doubt the authenticity of the extract.

[2] The Latin text is given in Hamelius, II, p.5.

duties coincided with his. Long afterwards, and in a place far removed from thence, namely in the city of Liége, by his advice and with the assistance of this venerable man, I composed this treatise, as I shall relate more fully at the end of the whole book.

The sequel follows in chapter L.

In the year 1355 from the birth of our Lord Jesus Christ on my way home, I stayed in the noble city of Liége. I fell sick there with disease and arthritic gout in a district called Basse Sauvenyr. In order to assure my recovery I consulted some physicians of that city, and it happened, by the grace of God, that there came to me one physician, more venerable than all the others by reason of his age and his grey hair, evidently skilful in his art, who was there called Master John with the Beard. In the course of conversation together he made some observations, as a result of which we renewed our former acquaintance in Cairo, in Egypt, in the castle of the sultan Calahelich, which I touched on in chapter VII of this book. When he had proved the knowledge of his art for my benefit, he exhorted and prayed me forthwith that I should write down some part of what I had seen during my wanderings through this world, so that it might be read and heard for the benefit of posterity. So at last, by his advice and aid, this treatise was written, although I had not intended to write anything until I had at last reached my own country in England. And I believe that all that happened to me happened by providence and the grace of God. For since the time of my departure our two kings of England and France have not ceased to wage war, with destructions, depredations, ambushes and slaughter, in the course of which, unless I had been under God's protection, I could not have escaped without death or the danger of death, or the accumulation of great evils. Now, thirty-three years after my departure, living in the city of Liége, which lies only two day's journey from the English Channel, I have learnt that, by God's grace, the aforesaid lords have made an end of their enmity. Wherefore I hope and intend for the rest of my old age to be able to give heed to my body's comfort and the salvation of my soul. Here then is the end of my writing.

As Sir George Warner points out, it may be inferred that this passage was not written as early as 1355, since it appears to refer to the Peace of Bretigny of 1360, although possibly it may refer to the nominal truce for two years which followed the Battle of Poitiers in September, 1356.

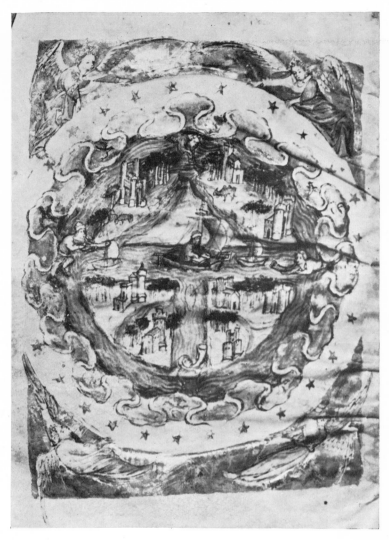

I. MANDEVILLE ON HIS TRAVELS

From a Dutch MS in the South African
Public Library, Cape Town.

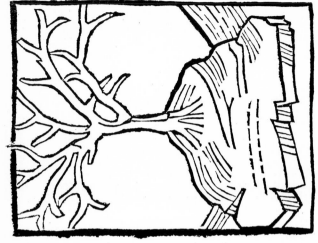

III. THE DRY TREE
From Velser's translation, 1482.
(See p. 47).

II. THE PYRAMIDS
(Joseph's Garners)
From Velser's translation, 1482
(See p. 46).

The various versions do not agree either as to the date of the setting out or the return. The Cotton version says that Mandeville returned in 1357, thirty-five years after he set out. This is the date in the earliest French MS. Other MSS, French and English, have as the date of return, 1356, or 1366 in the case of those which make Mandeville set out in 1332, while the Latin vulgate text has 1355 as the date of return. A short dedication to Edward III (not in the English versions) is given in some French MSS, and in the Latin vulgate, but this is probably a later addition.

The claim of St. Albans to show the traveller's burial place need not be seriously considered, although an inscription to this effect may still be seen in the Abbey, on the second pillar north of the west door. In fact, Mandeville was buried at Liége. His tomb was shown in the church of the Guillelmites, near Liége (destroyed in the French Revolution), and was seen by travellers whose reports extend from the fourteenth to the eighteenth century.

There are different versions of the inscription, but, as reconstructed and translated by Hamelius, it reads as follows: 'Here lies the noble lord Sir John of Mandeville, knight, otherwise named with the beard (*alias dictus ad Barbam*), lord of Campredi, born in England, practitioner of medicine and very pious in his prayers and very liberal in giving of his property to the poor. After viewing nearly all the world, he ended the last day of his life at Liége in the year of our Lord 1372, on November 17th.'[1] Hamelius refers also to two documents dealing with real property at Liége. A document dated 1386, describes 'Mestre Johan ale Barbe' as a former inmate of a house there, and another document, dated 1459, speaks of the same house where 'Mandavale the knight of England, who had been through all the world, used to dwell, who now lies in [the church of the] Guillemins.'[2]

---

[1] Hamelius (II, p. 1), quoting from a fifteenth-century writer, gives February 7th, but other writers agree on November 17th.

[2] Gobert, *Les Rues de Liége* (1901), IV, pp. 201-3.

The epitaph was apparently engraved on stone with a coat of arms (which did not represent the arms of any branch of the Mandeville family), and the monks showed the traveller's saddle, spurs and bridle-bit,[1] also two great knives which Mandeville is said to have used on his travels.

There is, so far, one other link in the chain. A French MS copied for Charles V of France in 1371,[2] one year before the date inscribed on Mandeville's tomb, which contains the earliest known copy of the travels, was originally bound up with a treatise on the plague written by 'Jehan de Bourgoigne autrement dit à la Barbe, professeur en médicin et cytoien du Liége,' in 1365, and copied by the same scribe. This conjunction of the two names can hardly be accidental.

On these facts, and apart from a half-hearted attempt in the Latin vulgate text to split the identity, there can be no doubt that Mandeville and de Bourgogne were one and the same person. If the evidence of identification rested solely on Outremeuse there might be some doubt, for Outremeuse is an unsatisfactory witness and it may well be that he did not tell the whole truth. But fortunately there is other evidence. We have confirmation in the inscription on the tomb, and local tradition supports it. Moreover, there was a John de Mandeville who was concerned in 1312 in the death of Piers Gaveston and was pardoned in 1313. A Sir John de Burgoyne took part in the rising against the Despensers in 1321, in the reign of Edward II. He was pardoned, but, except that his pardon was revoked, we know little about him. John de Mandeville was not apparently involved in these events, but as an enemy of the Despensers he would have been a partisan of de Bourgogne,

---

[1] Warner p. xxxii, and John Ray (1663), II, p. 51 (ed. of 1738), not noticed by Warner. Louis Abry, the Liége herald, says that Mandeville left his library to the Guillemins, whom he made his heirs. If this is so the will referred to by Outremeuse was probably destroyed with the church. Warner, p. xxxvi.

[2] Some account of this beautiful and interesting MS is given in the Bibliography (No. 34).

and may well have taken his name in 1322, which is the year when Mandeville in his 'Travels' professes to have left England. Having killed a man of birth, Mandeville would naturally be anxious to go into hiding. The difficulty here is that if the Mandeville who was a soldier in 1312 was the author of the 'Travels,' he must have been a *very* old man when he died sixty years later. A recent writer, Mr. Isaac Jackson, claims to have found a fresh answer to this perplexing conundrum.[1] He has discovered that the Mandevilles of Twescard, North Antrim, murdered their lord, Wm. de Burgh, Earl of Ulster, in 1333, and that the fatal blow was struck by Sir John Mandeville of Donnahir, or Donnegore. It is suggested that this Irish Sir John fled to Liége, and went disguised as a pilgrim to the Holy Land, and that the date, 1322, given in some versions as the date of the commencement of the 'Travels,' was inserted deliberately in order to establish an alibi if Mandeville was accused of a murder in 1333. It is an interesting theory, but, unfortunately, there is nothing to connect the author of the 'Travels' with Ireland.

We are now faced by a very pretty muddle which has puzzled wiser heads than mine. But I believe that we have two important clues in the nickname *à la barbe* and in the practice of medicine. It is scarcely to be credited that two men living in the same town and closely associated with each other should both have been called *à la barbe*, and as to the practice of medicine, a work *de Pestilentia*, attributed to John de Bourgogne *with the beard*, but which may very possibly have been written by Mandeville, was very well-known and had a wide public both here and on the continent.[2]

According to Outremeuse, Mandeville was skilled in medicine. Oxford possesses several manuscript treatises on

---

[1] See *Modern Language Review* (1928), p. 466.
[2] See *The Black Book of Paisley*, by D. Murray (1885), pp. 80, 88, and the same writer's *John de Burdaeus or John de Burgundia, otherwise Sir John Mandeville, and the Pestilence* (1891).

alchemy by Johannes de Magna Villa, and, in 1564, there was said to be extant at Antwerp a work by Mandeville *de re medica*.[1] A contemporary of Mandeville, the chronicler Radulphus de Rivo, Dean of Tongres, who died in 1403, calls Mandeville *vir ingenio et arte medendi eminens*. Another chronicler of a slightly later date, Cornelius Zantfliet, a Benedictine of St. Jacques at Liége, who compiled a chronicle covering the years 1230 to 1461, speaks of Mandeville as *aliter cum barba*, and *in arte medicinae peroptime tritus*.[2] It was as John *with the beard*, otherwise Sir John Mandeville, a physician, that de Bourgogne disclosed himself on his death-bed to Outremeuse, and it is as Sir John Mandeville *with the beard*, practitioner of medicine that he was buried.

But there are two other important factors which seem to me to be conclusive. First, in the 'Travels,' after describing the Arabic alphabet, the author remarks that *we in England* have two extra letters in our a b c, namely þ and ȝ 'which be clept thorn and ȝogh' and this passage, be it noted, is not confined to the English versions. The book as a whole gives the impression that the author was an Englishman and surely no one but an Englishman could have written that. Secondly, we have the inscription on the tombstone. According to the eighteenth-century herald Abry, Mandeville made the Guillelmites his heirs, but, quite apart from this, I do not believe that a religious order, whether benefitting under the will or not, would have allowed a lying inscription to appear on a tombstone in its church. There were no doubt masses to be said for the soul of the deceased benefactor. Whose soul were the brothers to pray for? Obviously Mandeville's and not de Bourgogne's. The more the problem is studied the clearer it becomes, at least to my mind, that Mandeville was a man of flesh and blood, born, as he says, at St. Albans, that he practised medicine and was known to his contemporaries as the man with the

---

[1] Murray, op. cit., p. 89.   [2] Warner, p. xxxiv.

beard, that he fled the country, and that de Bourgogne was a name invented or borrowed by Mandeville to conceal his identity.[1]

I realise that I have here a whole concensus of learned opinion against me, but where there is so much uncertainty one guess is as good as another. Although I have plunged into the controversy myself, I feel that far too much paper and ink have been expended on the problem. After all these centuries it is the man as disclosed in his book that is important, not the man himself. The man himself can now never be anything but a ghost.

The book — whether by Mandeville or de Bourgogne — is believed to have been written after 1360. The year 1366 has been suggested.[2] It was long believed that it was written in Latin, and then translated by the author into French and out of French into English, 'that every man of my nation may understand it,' a statement which occurs (so far as is known) only in the standard English version (Cotton MS Titus C.xvi). This is flatly contradicted by the earliest French version of 1371. Here the passage reads: 'Sachies que ie eusse cest livret mis en latin pour plus briefment deviser. Mais pource que pluseurs entendent mieulx rommant que latin, ie l'ay mis en rommant, par quoy que chascun lentende.' (Know that I *should have* put this book into Latin to be more concise, but seeing that many understand Romance (French) better than Latin, I have put it into Romance, to the end that everyone may understand it).[3] The first to draw attention to this was the

---

[1] Unfortunately nothing can be made of the dedication to Edward III. It does not appear in any known English version, where one would naturally look for it, but only in some inferior French MSS.

[2] See article by Arpad Steiner in *Speculum* (1934) IX, p. 145.

[3] It is interesting to see how the passage fared at the hands of the different translators. The Italian version states that the book was composed 'in vulgare,' the Dutch that it was written in "Duutsch." Velser writes that the book was 'made in French, since not everybody speaks *German* or understands Latin.' Von Diemeringen merely states that the book was written in French. The Spanish translator omits the passage altogether.

French scholar M. d'Avezec, in 1839, but E. W. B. Nicholson afterwards Bodley's Librarian, restated the evidence in a letter to *The Academy*, on 11 November, 1876. He was contemplating an edition of Mandeville (which unfortunately did not appear). He showed conclusively that the book was originally written in French, and that the Latin and English versions were made by unknown translators. Moreover, all the known English MSS, except the Cotton and Egerton versions, and the two English versions at the Bodleian referred to later, omit a long passage in the description of Egypt. This passage occupies twenty-six pages in Halliwell's reprint of 1839 and must have been due to carelessness on the part of the translator, unless he worked from a defective French text. In any event no author would have perpetrated such a glaring absurdity. There are also numerous blunders in the Cotton and other translations which no author would have passed. These are dealt with in some detail later (p. 145).

CHAPTER II

The Times

BEFORE we come to the journey itself, it may be well to sketch in outline the historical background against which Mandeville lived and wrote. During practically the whole period covered by the so-called travels England and France were at war. The Hundred Years' War broke out in 1338. Crécy was won in 1346, Calais was taken in 1347, and at Poitiers, in 1356, the French King was taken prisoner. Mandeville speaks in his Epilogue of the destruction and slaughter and the accumulations of evils produced by the war, and of the two kings having made peace, but writing, as he appears to have done, in his library at Liége, the struggle, under God's protection, left him untouched. Liége cannot, however, have been always a haven of rest. The town went through much the same domestic upheavals as other Flemish towns, and local disturbances must have figured largely in the daily life of the people, even if they left our author in peace.

During the whole of the century the hope of recovering the Holy Land was never absent from men's minds. The Crusade of 1270 led by Louis IX of France had ended in disaster, and Mandeville, like others, must have viewed the growing power of Islam with dismay. He refers again and again to the need for a new crusading spirit, but he realised that, unless Christian princes composed their differences and presented a united front with the Church, there was no hope of success. The Holy Land was lost by sin and could only be recovered by righteousness. But quite apart from the quarrels of princes, the affairs of the

Church were in such disorder that no joint effort was possible. Between 1305 and 1378 the popes were at Avignon. The Franciscans were demanding evangelical poverty for the pope and all churchmen. They denounced the wealth and splendour of the papal court and were preparing the way for Wycliffe. Mandeville makes no effort to conceal his feelings about the papacy, but he was probably only reflecting the views of thousands of others. There is no reason to believe that his anti-papal feelings affected his general outlook or disturbed his peace of mind.

There was one event, however, which must have gravely affected our author's tranquility — the Black Death, which decimated Europe from 1347 onwards. There is no reference to this in the 'Travels,' but Mandeville, alias de Bourgogne, lived through it. He speaks of himself in his *de Pestilentia* as having practised medicine for forty years, and refers to his experiences at Liége during one outbreak which raged there in 1356.

Mandeville knew what he was doing when he sat down to write a book of travels, for during the first part of the fourteenth century, travel was in the air.[1] The Polos had returned to Venice in 1295 from their long sojourn in Asia, and for the next fifty years, that is roughly between 1290 and 1340, a steady stream of travellers took the eastern road. The Tartar conquests of the first part of the thirteenth century had accomplished one of the most striking revolutions in history, by bringing the East into touch with the West. In 1214 the Tartars swept from Mongolia upon China, taking Peking and conquering most of Eastern Asia. They then turned westward, spread across Asia and over a large part of Russia, into Poland, Hungary and Persia, so that by 1259 one empire extended from the Yellow River to the banks of the Danube, and from the Persian Gulf to Siberia. At first Europe was horror-struck by the invasion.

[1] On the whole subject see the brilliant chapter by the late Eileen Power, 'Routes to Cathay' in *Travel and Travellers of the Middle Ages* (1926), ed. Newton.

It seemed as if the end of the world was at hand, and that Gog and Magog and the armies of anti-Christ had at last burst forth from their mountain fastnesses to destroy Christianity and overrun the whole world. Then, after much hesitation and confusion of mind, it dawned upon the West that, horrible and brutal as the conquerors were, they might be useful as allies in breaking down the power of Islam. The Tartars were known to be tolerant of all creeds. The first thing was to convert them to Christianity, and then, with their help, to recover the Holy land. It was a vain hope, but it produced a wave of missionary zeal which is one of the glories of the medieval Church — the episode of the missionary friars. There are few brighter or more romantic stories in history than the tale of the journeys, successes and failures of the Christian pioneers in Asia. But, although the best travel-books were written by missionaries — Mandeville makes use of two of them — the real impetus to travel was given by trade, and it was by the trade-routes that merchants took the road to Cathay. The journey must have been hazardous enough, according to modern ideas, but the merchants seem to have made light of it. They appear to have penetrated everywhere in the East. Luckily, we know a good deal about their journeys and the difficulties they had to face from the *Pratica della Mercatura*,[1] a kind of merchants' handbook, written about 1340 by Pegolotti, an agent of the great Florentine house of Bardi. The book deals with the trade between the Levant and the East, and describes the route from Tana to Peking, with all kinds of practical suggestions for the novice. He must let his beard grow and hire a dragoman at Tana. His servants must speak Kuman and he would be wise to take a Kuman woman with him if he wished to study his comfort, although comfort is a strange word to use when one realizes that the journey was likely to

[1] Extracts in Yule's *Cathay and the Way Thither*, Hakluyt Society, second ed. vol. III.

take some six or seven months (Mandeville says eleven or twelve months from Venice or Genoa to Cathay), travelling at times with ox-wagons, camel-carts and pack-asses, with only outlying and remote halting places for rest and refreshment. One of the most striking commentaries on medieval commercial intercourse is the statement by Pegolotti that the road from Tana to Peking was perfectly safe whether by day or night, but this must surely be an overstatement. Mandeville has several references to merchants, but he never makes light of their difficulties.

Mandeville's ideas of geography were those of his age. By his time geography had lost its character of a science and had become once more the subject of myth and fancy. In the Middle Ages there were two schools of geographical thought, the ecclesiastical or patristic, and the Arabic. The Arabs' approach to geography was scientific, speculative and progressive. The ecclesiastical outlook was traditional, stereotyped and hide-bound by authority, and it is with this school that we are concerned. The Fathers of the Church would have nothing to do with original thought. For them the Ptolemaic writings and the studies of Arabic geographers might never have existed. Nothing could be sanctioned which had not the authority of Holy Writ. This clerical hold on scholarship was responsible, among others, for two conspicuous features of medieval geography — the belief that Jerusalem was the centre of the earth — 'I have set it in the midst of the nations' (Ezekiel V. 5) — and the situation of the Earthly Paradise. Both the Earthly Paradise and Jerusalem as the centre of the earth figure largely in Mandeville, as they do in all the medieval picture maps, and in the pilgrim and other geographical literature of the Middle Ages.

Taken as a whole, Mandeville's world was a circle enclosing a sort of T-square. The east was at the top. Jerusalem was plumb in the centre. The Mediterranean sea straggles across the lower half, which was divided between

Europe and Africa. The top was devoted to Asia, which was expanded to an enormous extent, and, as very little was known about it, the medieval map-makers filled up the blanks with monsters and other strange creatures which they took from the Bible, Crusaders' tales and other sources. If we want to know what Mandeville's world looked like we have only to examine the great *Mappa Mundi* in Hereford Cathedral which was made about 1300. The T-square fits into it perfectly. The Earthly Paradise is at the top. Jerusalem is in the centre, and here and there, particularly in Africa, are pictures of all the strange monsters described by Mandeville, with their idiosyncracies pithily set forth in crabbed Latin legends. I shall have more to say about this map later, but the resemblance between it and Mandeville's notion of geography is too marked to be overlooked.

Mandeville had no doubt that the world was round, that its circumference was 20,425 miles (or more) and that in the heart and midst of it was Jerusalem. There could be no doubt about this, for men could prove and shew it 'by a spear that is pight into the earth, upon the hour of mid-day, when it is equinox, that sheweth no shadow on no side,' which seems to imply that the Holy City was on the equator ! Mandeville was concerned about the antipodes because of the suggestion (by the supporters of the flat-earth theory) that, if the earth were in fact a sphere, the men on the sides and lower surface would be living side-ways or upside down, even if they did not fall off into space, and, if men could fall off the earth, there was no reason why the great globe itself (being so great and heavy) should not topple over into the void, which was of course unthinkable. 'But that may not be, and therefore saith our Lord God, *Non timeas me, qui suspendi terram ex nihilo.*' Moreover, as Mandeville implies, if a man thinks he is walking upright he is in fact walking the right way up, as God meant him to do, and that is all that matters.

As to the roundness of the earth, it was beyond all question, for in his youth Mandeville had heard tell of a worthy man who went so far by sea and land that he came at last to an island where, to his amazement, he heard a ploughman calling to his beasts in his own language. The traveller had encompassed the whole earth without knowing it.

To these observations the author adds some sensible remarks on the way in which astronomers apply mathematical reasoning to the mapping of the firmament and the earth. These observations, and his familiarity with the use of the astrolabe, suggest that he was not only abreast of, but actually at times in advance of, the scientific knowledge of his time.

CHAPTER III

Mandeville's Predecessors

MANDEVILLE's book is, of course, a compilation, and, thanks to the brilliant detective work done by Sir George Warner and Dr. Bovenschen, we know a great deal about the sources from which the book was compiled. Mandeville's great standby was the vast encyclopedia of Vincent of Beauvais (d. 1264). Vincent is best known by his *Speculum Mundi*, a huge work divided into four parts, with the titles *Naturale*, *Doctrinale*, *Historiale* and *Morale* (the last being probably spurious). Vincent's reading must have been prodigious. In the *Speculum Naturale* he cites 350 authors, with 100 more in the *Specula Doctrinale* and *Historiale*. This work was first printed in 1473 in ten (or seven) folio volumes, but the edition generally used is the Douai edition of 1624 in four volumes entitled *Bibliotheca Mundi*, in which each of the *Specula* is contained in a huge folio volume. This work was Mandeville's storehouse of learning. It contained copious extracts from the travels of the Franciscan Carpini, referred to later, while the quotations from Pliny, Solinus, Jerome, Isidore of Seville, the Alexander romances and the early Bestiaries supplied Mandeville with his notions of geography, his fabulous monsters, and other strange odds and ends of natural history. We shall probably never know the full extent of Mandeville's indebtedness to Vincent, but in some 140 pages of the Cotton version printed by Pollard I have counted between forty and fifty passages which can be traced directly or indirectly to this source, and there must be many others which cannot now be identified.

The two great missionary travellers of the Middle Ages were John de Plano Carpini and Odoric of Pordenone. Carpini, a Franciscan, set out from Lyons in 1245 with a letter from the Pope. He reached the Great Chan's camp in July 1246, having ridden something like 3,000 miles in 106 days. He was well received, and returned safely to Lyons in 1247, bringing with him the Great Chan's reply to the Pope. Carpini cannot have been less than sixty-five years of age when he set out. He was very fat, and such were the hardships he suffered on his journey that he died from their effects. His book is in many ways the most important record of overland expansion before Marco Polo. It first revealed the Mongol world to Christendom, and its account of Mongol manners, customs and history is invaluable. Mandeville's debt to Carpini has already been mentioned.

Friar Odoric of Pordenone left for the East between 1316 and 1318, by the long sea route from Ormuz to Canton, stopping by the way in India, Ceylon, Sumatra, Java and Borneo. From Canton he went by land to Zaiton and on to Kinsai, finally reaching Cambalech (Peking) and the court of the Great Chan by the Grand Canal. He spent three years at Peking, returning by a land route which may have included a visit to Lhasa. The extent to which Mandeville pillaged the book did not increase Odoric's reputation for truth, but Odoric does not merit the charge of mendacity which has been launched against him. He was an honest and original observer, and his errors are those of an eyewitness. What version of Odoric was used by Mandeville is not known, but, so far as Carpini is concerned, everything which Mandeville wanted was in Vincent of Beauvais' Encyclopedia.[1]

Mandeville must also have had access to the travels of another missionary friar, William of Rubruck, who went to Tartary under orders from St. Louis (Louis IX) of France in 1251, but only one episode has been traced to that

[1] *Spec. Hist.* Bk. XXXI, ch. 3-52: Douai ed. IV, p. 1,286–1,303.

source, the story of the monk who climbed to the top of
Mount Ararat and brought down a plank from the Ark,
which was still preserved there. It is a pity that Mandeville
did not make more use of this entertaining book, for
Rubruck's narrative is full of intimate little personal details
which make a story live. Mandeville had by him also the
Fleur des Histoires d'Orient, by Haiton (or Heyton) the
younger (d. 1308), a member of the royal house of Armenia,
whose work deals with the geography of Asia and with
the history of Egypt and the Tartars. We shall see later
how this important narrative is dovetailed into Mandeville's
book, but it is sufficient to say here that the chapter, 'Wherefore he is called the Great Chan,' is taken almost literally
from Haiton. Mandeville's account of the Amazons must
have come from a variety of sources, but in the Egerton
version he takes at least one name from Dante's tutor
Brunetto Latini (d. 1294), whose *Livres deu Tresor* supplied
Mandeville with one passage on Gog and Magog and the
enclosed people shut up behind the Caspian Mountains.
Ricold of Monte Croce (d. 1320), another missionary
friar, fills in a gap left by Carpini in the account of Tartar
customs and beliefs with the story of the Tartars' veneration for the owl. Mandeville also makes considerable
use of Jacques de Vitry, whose history, written about the
year 1218, provides, among other matters, a lengthy description of the Greek Church. Mandeville did not think as
highly of Prester John as he did of the Great Chan, but he
has much to say about this elusive and mysterious potentate,
and of the wonders and marvels to be found in his dominions. Here Mandeville used the famous forged Letter
which began to circulate in Europe about the year 1165.
This Letter, as we have it now, has a number of interpolations which appear to have accumulated from time to
time under the hands of succeeding copyists. What text
Mandeville used is not known, but the whole subject of
Mandeville's use of the letter has been studied by Professor

Zarncke,[1] and is too complicated to be discussed here. It is sufficient for us to know that Mandeville did use the Letter, and use it freely.

The first part of Mandeville's book, which purports to be a kind of guide for pilgrims to the Holy Land, is to my mind the least interesting. It shows a curious lack of timing, and raises a doubt as to whether Mandeville was ever in the Holy Land at all. When he is not copying from Boldensele, a German knight who visited Palestine in 1332–3, he relies on earlier writers, who, in some instances at least, described the Holy Places before the capture of Jerusalem by Saladin in 1187. Except that it is packed with Bible stories, this part of the book must have been quite useless to fourteenth-century pilgrims. The earlier travellers Eugesippus (c. 1155), John of Würzburg (c. 1165), and Theodoric (c. 1172) appear to have used a standard travel manual called the Old Compendium which is now lost, although it is quite possible that Mandeville had access to it. But he takes little or no trouble to bring his material up to date. His route to Constantinople through Hungary, as well as the route through Asia Minor, is taken from the history of the First Crusade written by Albert of Aix some 250 years earlier. One of the most popular and authoritative pilgrim-books of the period was the itinerary of Burchard of Mount Sion (c. 1283), but there is no evidence to show that Mandeville knew of it, except in so far as it was adapted by later writers. Mandeville did use, however, a book on the Holy Land, the *Liber de Terra Sancta*, attributed to Odoric, whose eastern travels he pillaged freely in the latter part of his book. Other pilgrim-writers of note, whose books might have passed through Mandeville's hands, although there is no direct evidence to show that they did, are Saewulf (1102), Thietmar (1217), Symon Simeonis (1321–22), and Ludolph of Sudheim (1336). Symon Simeonis, Ludolph and Boldensele are the outstanding

[1] 'Der Priester Johannes', II, p. 128. See Bibliography under Zarncke.

IV. NOAH'S ARK ON MOUNT ARARAT
From a MS in the Bibliothèque Nationale, Paris.
(See p. 53).

V. THE GREAT CHAN AT TABLE
From a MS in the Bibliothèque Nationale, Paris.
(See p. 66).

VI. ST. THOMAS' HAND

From a MS in the Bibliothèque Nationale, Paris.

(See p. 59).

pilgrim-writers of the fourteenth century. Their records are based on personal observation and are amusing and authoritative. Mandeville, as we know, copied from Boldensele. If he had used the other two he might have produced a really useful guide-book.

CHAPTER IV

Truth or Fiction

IT IS NOT easy to trace the development of modern criticism concerning Mandeville, and it is strange how the pendulum swings to and fro. An air of verisimilitude was undoubtedly given by the statement in the English versions that Mandeville, on his way home, submitted his book to the pope at Rome, and that the holy father approved of it, but this passage does not appear in any of the French manuscripts and is clearly an interpolation. For most contemporary readers the book had to rest on its own foundations, and as the marvels which Mandeville sets down as sober facts can be capped and even outrivalled by other writers — the author of Prester John's Letter, for instance — the reading public of the fourteenth and fifteenth centuries probably swallowed their Mandeville whole. Bale, who published his *Catalogue of British Writers* in 1548, had no doubt about the authenticity of the 'Travels,' and his contemporary Leland (who died in 1552), goes even further, for he placed Mandeville above Marco Polo, Columbus, and Cortez and other travellers (*nemo tamen illorum tamdiu labori insistebat, quam noster Magnovillanus*), and he compares Mandeville with Mithridates for his knowledge of foreign languages.[1] Leland tells us that as a boy he heard much about Mandeville from an old man called Jordan, and that at Canterbury he had seen among the relics at Becket's shrine a crystal orb containing an apple, still undecayed — an offering, so he was told, from Mandeville himself.

---

[1] Bishop Tanner's *Bibliotheca Britannico-Hibernica* (1748), p. 505, quoted by Warner, p. 31.

Purchas[1] thought Mandeville 'the greatest Asian Traveller that ever the World had,' and accused some other writer (probably a friar) of having stuffed his book full of fables. He placed Mandeville next (if next) to Marco Polo, and accused Odoric, who really was a great Asiatic traveller, of thieving from Mandeville, whereas in fact the substance of Mandeville's travels in India and Cathay was stolen without acknowledgement from Odoric. As we shall see, Mandeville, in his account of his adventures in the Valley Perilous, states that among his companions were two friars minor from Lombardy. The whole passage is worked up from Friar Odoric, and the reference to the two friars may well have been intended to anticipate a possible charge of plagiarism, and to suggest that Mandeville and Odoric travelled together. The result can be seen in a manuscript at Wolfenbüttel of the *Liber de Terra Sancta*, attributed to Odoric, which begins: 'Itinerarius fidelis fratris Oderici, *socii militis Mandavil*, per Indiam, licet hic prius et alter posterius peregrinationem suam descripsit.'[2] As Sir George Warner points out, the friar is doubly wronged here by the assertion that Mandeville's work was written first, whereas Odoric's was written in 1330. It may be noted that in the Antwerp (Gouda) Latin edition of Mandeville, printed in 1485 (and reprinted in the first edition of Hakluyt), frequent references to Odoric have been inserted in the text, and the description of the Valley Perilous ends with a statement that Odoric did not suffer as much there as Mandeville. The whole subject is discussed later (p. 89).

But poor Odoric was to suffer still greater indignities at a later date. In the collection of travels called 'Astley's Voyages' published in 1745–7 Odoric's narrative is described as superficial and full of lies, and in the index he

---

[1] *His Pilgrimes* (1625), reprint XI, pp. 188, 364.
[2] Warner, p. 22. Cf. Yule, *Cathay and the Way Thither*, II, p. 45, who refers to another MS at Mainz with the same opening statement.

fares even worse, his name being entered as 'Odoric, Friar, Travels of, IV, 620.[1] A great Liar.'

There is a curious Mandeville reference in the English translation of Estienne's *Apology for Herodotus*, 1607, by R. Carew. In his Introduction to the Reader, the translator writes: 'imagine not that thou hast either . . . Goularts Admiranda, or Wolfius his Memorabilia, or Torquemeda's Mandevile of Miracles, or any such rhapsodie of an indigested history.' This last reference is to the "Jardin de Flores Curiosas" by Antonio de Torquemada, 1570 translated by Ferdinando Walker as "The Spanish Mandevile of Miracles," 1600.'

But the English title is not quite fair either to the Spanish author or to Mandeville. The book is a curious but amusing hotch-potch of monsters, the vagaries of fortune, strange countries, dreams, spirits, witches and hags, mostly from Spanish sources, such as Robert Burton would have loved. There is a good deal about the Earthly Paradise, Cathay and Prester John. Mandeville is mentioned here and there, and we learn with interest, what Sir John does not tell us, that he received wages and a pension from the Great Chan, but most of the eastern stories come from Marco Polo. The translator seems to have done his work well and does not appear to have added anything of his own, nor is there anything in his Dedication to explain the title-page. All we can say is that he must have been reflecting the views of his contemporaries.

Neither Robert Burton nor Sir Thomas Browne subscribed to Purchas's opinion of Mandeville. The former dismisses Mandeville quite briefly as a liar.[1] It does not appear from the list of Burton's books at the Bodleian and Christ Church that he even possessed a copy of the 'Travels.'[2]

---

[1] *Anatomy of Melancholy*, ed. Shilleto, II, p. 46. But then Burton also calls Marco Polo a liar.

[2] Oxford Bibliographical Society, *Proceedings*, I pt. III, 1925, p. 224 ff.

Sir Thomas Browne says much the same but in more temperate language.[1] The writer on Mandeville in Chalmer's *Biographical Dictionary* (1815), asserts that many things in the book, which were looked on as fabulous for a long time, had then been verified beyond all doubt, but giving up his giants of fifty feet high, there did not appear to be any very good reason why Sir John should not be believed in things that he relates from his own observation, and this seems to be the line taken generally in the eighteenth century. But it is difficult to know what is meant by personal observation. Mandeville claims in his Prologue to have visited all the countries he mentions, and the not infrequent interjections — 'This I saw not': 'I was not there' and so on — imply that he saw and experienced whatever else he describes; but in Pollard's edition, containing 209 pages, I have counted only twenty-three specific personal statements — I saw, I dwelt, I came, I departed, I asked, and so on. And of these, one at least, the passage through the Valley Perilous, required a good deal of justification at the hands of the German translator, Velser, before it could be presented to his readers.[2] Hugh Murray, in the early nineteenth century, was shrewd enough to realise that much of Mandeville was lifted from Odoric and others and had no hesitation in pronouncing the work to be pure and entire fabrication — 'What he added of his own consists, I think, quite exclusively of monstrous lies.'[3] We can cap this with a quotation from an old Play:[4]

'Drake was a didapper to Mandevill.
Candish and Hawkins, Frobisher, all our Voyagers
Went short of Mandevill.'

But shortly after Murray's indictment an anonymous

[1] 'Vulgar Errors,' in *Works*, ed. Wilkin, II, p. 236.   [2] See below, p. 92.
[3] *Historical Account of Discoveries and Travels* (1820), I, ch. iv.
[4] Quoted by Beazley, *Dawn of Modern Geography*, III, p. 322.

writer was busy compiling a long justification of Mandeville, which appeared in the *Retrospective Review* for 1821, vol. III, part II, p. 269. The writer protests in no uncertain terms against the great outcry of fraud which had been raised against Mandeville. There was no question of falsehood. All that could be charged against him was want of judgment. The writer's concluding words are worth quoting. 'The literature of the middle ages has scarcely a more entertaining and interesting subject; and to an Englishman it is doubly valuable, as establishing the title of his country to claim as its own the first example of the liberal and independent gentleman, travelling over the world in the disinterested pursuit of knowledge unsullied in his reputation; honored and respected wherever he went for his talents and personal accomplishments.' Curiously enough, this is much the line taken by Halliwell in his Introduction to the 1839 reprint of the Travels. And so matters remained until the 1870's when Nicholson laid the foundations for a new approach to the whole subject in his letter to *The Academy* on 11 November, 1876. His subsequent letters appeared in that journal on 12 February, 1881 and 12 April, 1884.

But whether truth or fiction, Mandeville's influence on the literature of the sixteenth century was profound. Many of his stories and most of his monsters, as depicted by his artists, found their way into the *Nuremberg Chronicle*, and Münster's *Cosmographia* (1544). Like the *Nuremberg Chronicle*, Münster's book was extremely popular, there having been as many as forty-seven editions in seven languages before 1650.

Münster was a very learned person. He had 120 collaborators to help him in his work, and when he wrote there was already a considerable literature in existence with which he was perfectly familiar, and to which he could have turned for an accurate and sober account of late geographical discovery. But, so far as Asia, India and Africa are concerned, he made little use of this material. Instead, we have the old stories and pictures of cannibals, one-eyed, one-legged and headless men, Amazons, pigmies and Brahmans, dragons, unicorns, gold-digging ants and griffins. Münster does not mention Mandeville by name (he acknowledges his debt to Marco Polo and Haiton, the Armenian), but it was Mandeville who created the popular demand for stories of this kind, and it was a demand which had to be met.

There can be no doubt that this demand was increased by the great discoveries of the fifteenth and sixteenth centuries. Eastward and westward by 1530, the route lay open to the Indies, and although the English at first had troubled little about conquest and the planting of colonies, the foreign press teemed with accounts of the New World and the East, and each returning traveller added something fresh. Münster's *Cosmographia* was abridged and translated into English in 1552, and in 1564 appeared a curious and interesting book which showed that the English were not to be outdone in the hue and cry after wonders and marvels. This was *A Dialogue against the Fever pestilence* by Wm. Bullein, a man of learning and a physician. Bullein had obviously read and studied Mandeville, Münster and any other books of travel he could come across, and he disliked and distrusted what he read — and a good many other things as well. But he did a very dangerous thing. He satirised travel literature as a whole.

The result, which Bullein cannot have foreseen, is that his book owed any popularity it may have had, not to his attacks on usury, lawyers, legacy-hunters and the Church of Rome, not even to his timely and suitable remarks on fresh air, diet, and herbs as remedies for the plague, but to the introduction into his dialogues of a traveller called Mendax, one of the most amusing and attractive liars in literature. The name Mendax, we learn, signifies 'in the Ethiope tongue, the name of a great Citie, the mother of holie religion and truth,' and once the reader has met Mendax his interest never flags. It would be out of place here to follow Mendax in his travels in the East, diverting as they are, but it is sufficient to say that, among other adventures, he was turned into a dog (only temporarily), whereas his boy, a gentleman of good house, and would have married with one Jone Trim, was so strongly bewitched that he was a dog still. Most of Mandeville's stories re-appear, including the loadstone rocks, which Mandeville saw afar off, but on which Mendax and his companions were wrecked, escaping with their lives but losing their treasure.

Mandeville has much to say about the Antipodes. It was reserved for Mendax to discover there, foot against foot, another England, where were 'Gaddes Hill, Stangate Hole, Newe Market Heath, like ours in all points,' with this exception that, whereas there one found honest men, here there were none at all. We read of dancing geese, of parrots playing chess with apes and discoursing in Greek or singing descant, of Solomon and the Queen of Sheba seen in a magic mirror, attended by 14,000 ladies, and a race of men who cast their skins like snakes: 'Marie,' says he, 'they were full of hooles.' Here we have lying reduced to a fine art, but what Bullein did not realise was that the English have always loved a good liar and that satire is a two-edged weapon. It is possible that his book actually increased the demand for tall stories instead of killing it. In any event Mandeville continued to sell. A popular English edition with woodcuts appeared in 1568. In the eighteenth century the 'Travels' appeared as a chap-book. The sales went on all through the nineteenth century and its popularity has never waned, whereas Bullein's satire is now almost entirely forgotten.

BOOK TWO

The Journey

*

CHAPTER V

The Near East

MANDEVILLE's book is divided into two parts. Part I purports to be a guide to the Holy Land, which all men ought to love and cherish, and which they were in duty bound to reconquer. All possible routes are described, including one via Turkestan. The mention of saints and relics serves to introduce a number of Biblical and some most un-Biblical stories, and after a description of Mount Sinai and Egypt, the second portion of the book transports the reader to the Far East, where the author's imagination has full scope. It is possible that Mandeville did visit Palestine and Egypt, but there is little evidence to support this view. It has been suggested recently[1] that Mandeville's book was a work of propaganda aimed at inspiring a new crusading spirit. It is true that the hope of recovering the Holy Land was very near to Mandeville's heart. He gives a whole list of alternative routes and devotes special attention to the roads leading to Jerusalem from the Syrian coast towns. He also provides statistics as to the size of the Mameluke forces, and remarks that, if the water supply of Alexandria were cut off, the town could not withstand a siege. But the military statistics are quite unreliable. They are taken from Haiton (who wrote in 1307), and in one case the figures are

[1] A. S. Atiya, *The Crusade in the Later Middle Age* (1938), p. 163.

41

merely doubled, while the statement about Alexandria is too obvious to be of any military value. I do not believe that Mandeville had any definite idea of propaganda in his mind, or that he imagined for a moment that his book would be of any practical use to men of action. He was concerned only with the needs of pilgrims and the preservation of the Holy Places. If he was conscious of any other purpose when he sat down to write his book, he soon tired of it, for only sixteen chapters are devoted to the Near East and the Holy Land, whereas thirty-six are scarcely sufficient to describe the wonders and marvels of India, Cathay and the land of Prester John.

Chapter 1 brings us to Constantinople and describes the equestrian statue of Justinian which stood in the Forum Augusteum from 543 to 1550. According to Mandeville, the statue had formerly a golden apple in the right hand, but it had fallen down. 'And men say there that it is a token that the emperor hath lost a great part of his lands and of his lordships; for he was wont to be Emperor of Roumania and of Greece, of all Asia the less, and of the land of Syria, of the land of Judea, in the which is Jerusalem, and of the land of Egypt, of Persia, and of Arabia. But he hath lost all but Greece, and that land he holds all only. And men would many times put the apple into the image's hand again, but it will not hold it. This apple betokeneth the lordship that he had over all the world, that is round. And the tother hand he lifteth up against the East, in token to menace the misdoers.'

The bulk of this comes from the *Itinerary* of the German nobleman William of Boldensele, who visited Constantinople and the Holy Land in 1332–3, but when Boldensele was there the apple was still in the right hand, as it was as late as 1420. In 1317 the cross on the orb in the left hand was blown down, and Mandeville may have confused his references. At Constantinople was also the true Cross, and this leads to a disquisition on the wood from which it was made (which may well have come from the *Golden Legend*), followed by a description of the Crown of Thorns, which, with other relics, was sent to Paris in the time of St. Louis, King of France, and preserved thereafter in La Sainte Chapelle.

Chapter III contains a description of the windless summit of Mount Athos, which was so high that its shadow reached as far as Lemnos, seventy-six miles away. At the summit the air was so dry that neither man nor beast could live there, but some philosophers climbed to the top, holding wet sponges to their mouths, and wrote letters and figures with their fingers in the sand. A year later they went up again and found the letters and figures undisturbed. Substituting Olympus for Athos, this is taken with variations from Vincent of Beauvais: *Olympus . . . super quem literae inscriptae in pulvere per annum inventae sunt illaesae.*[1]

In chapter IV we have an account of the island of Cos (called Lango in the Middle Ages), where the daughter of Hypocras lived in the form and likeness of a dragon, and in this hideous shape she was to remain until a knight was so hardy as to kiss her on the mouth. Two unsuccessful attempts are described, but the source of the story has not been found. The description of Cyprus in chapter v seems to come from Boldensele. Here we have the story of the young man who desecrated the tomb of his lady love, and when he returned to the place after nine months, there flew out an adder (or a head), right hideous to see, which destroyed the city of Cathailye (Satalia: Adalia) and the country round about — a confused reference possibly to the legend of Medusa, which the crusaders may have brought home from the Holy Land. Here we have also the strange story of the lords and other men of Cyprus, who, on account of the great heat, dug trenches in the earth, deep to the knee, and sat there taking their meals in comfort. It was only at great feasts, or when strangers were entertained, that they set up

---

[1] *Spec. Nat.* VI. ch. 21.

forms and tables. No authority has been found for this story, although as Sir George Warner suggests, it may have something to do with the trenches dug by the Cypriots for the storage of their wine.

Egypt is described in chapters VI and VII from J. de Vitry, Haiton, the Armenian (c. 1307) and William of Tripoli (c. 1273). The list of sultans given in chapter VI is supplied by Haiton,[1] but here some independence is shown, for Haiton's list of sultans, which ends in 1300, is continued down to 1341, and in this chapter occurs a remark which may or may not be genuine: 'I ought right well to know it (the equipment of the sultan's household) for I dwelled with him as soldier in his wars a great while against the Bedouins.' But if this personal statement is to be believed it is odd that Mandeville adds nothing to the authorities he is using, except the statement that the Bedouins cooked their meat and fish by the rays of the sun. One would like to know how these nomads got their fish. It may well be, as Sir George Warner suggests (p. 18), that Mandeville simply inserted here what Vincent of Beauvais says about the Ichthyophagi of the Red Sea[2] *super petras solis calore ferventes assant pisces* and applied it to the Bedouins. It is just the kind of thing he would do. Chapter VII contains an amusing description of the phoenix and of the artificial incubation of chickens (almost literally from Boldensele). The apples of Paradise — 'and though ye cut them in never so many gobbets or parts overthwart or endlong, evermore ye shall find in the midst the figure of the Holy Cross' — are also taken from Boldensele, but the apples of Adam, which had a piece bitten out of the side, appear to come from Jacques de Vitry's *poma pulcherrima et citrina . . . in quibus quasi morsus hominis cum dentibus manifeste apparet, et idcirco poma Adami ab omnibus appellantur.*[3]

Next comes a description of the balsam garden at

---

[1] Book IV, ch. V–VII.   [2] *Spec. Hist.* I, ch. 86.
[3] Ed. Bongars in *Gesta Dei per Francos* (1611), p. 1099.

Materea, outside Cairo, which is taken largely from Boldensele, although the tests to be applied to tell whether the balm is counterfeit or true have a more respectable ancestry, and seem to go back to Pliny. This was the famous Garden where the Virgin Mary is said to have rested when she fled from the persecution of Herod. Mandeville tells us that the balsam was extracted from small trees 'that be none higher than to a man's breeks' girdle, and they seem as wood that is of the wild vine. And in that field be seven wells, that our Lord Jesu Christ made with one of his feet, when he went to play with the other children.' The branches could only be cut with a sharp flintstone or with a sharp bone, and the incision, as we learn from another traveller, had to be made by Christians. If cut with iron the balsam would be corrupted and the trees destroyed. We learn also, although not from Mandeville, that the oxen employed to draw water from the well refused to work on Sundays, which they observed as a day of rest. Mandeville, as we have seen, took his description from the German traveller Boldensele with details from other sources which cannot be traced, but every writer on Cairo has something to say about the Balsam Garden.[1]

It was said that the plant was procured by Cleopatra from Jericho, where it was formerly propagated from a root given to Solomon by the Queen of Sheba. The balm was a source of great wealth to the Sultan, who collected it in glass phials, which he presented, as if it were the greatest jewel in the world, to kings and princes. According to Ludolph the balm was good for wounds and hidden fractures of the limbs or body. It cured blindness, preserved dead bodies from corruption and fresh meat from decay.

The garden was destroyed during the disturbances in Cairo in 1496–97. When the German traveller, von Harff,

---

[1] We are fortunate in being able to fill in some of Mandeville's gaps from the reports of two contemporary travellers, the Irishman Symon Simeonis (1322), and Ludolph of Sudheim (1336). See Bibliography.

was there in 1497, the bushes had been pulled up and were lying on the ground, and it was said that no balsam could grow there for the next ten years.[1] Later travellers describe the garden as completely destroyed, but the Turks restored the garden, sending to Mecca, where the trees flourished in abundance, for fresh cuttings. In its heyday the garden must have been a delightful place, and distinguished travellers like Breydenbach, Dean of Mainz in 1483, were accustomed to rest there while waiting for the arrival of the dragoman who was to arrange for their entry into Cairo. The food was excellent (only the wine was very dear). The travellers could bathe in the spring and refresh themselves in a spacious house overlooking the garden, and enjoy the fragrant odours which were wafted through the windows, but these delights were reserved for fifteenth-century travellers.[2] It is doubtful whether any such amenities existed in Mandeville's time.

Like other medieval writers, Mandeville regards the Pyramids as Joseph's garners or barns, in which he stored up the corn against the lean years. Here Mandeville rejects Boldensele's sensible remarks as to their sepulchral nature, *dicunt simplices haec maxima monumenta fuisse granaria Pharaonis, et sic ea appellant. Sed nullo modo est . . .* Mandeville continues:

> And they be made of stone, full well made of masons' craft; of the which two be marvellously great and high, and the tother ne be not so great . . . And within they be all full of serpents. And above the garners without be many scriptures of diverse languages. And some men say that they be sepultures of great lords, that were sometime, but that is not true, for all the common rumour and speech is of all the people there, both far and near, that they be the garners of Joseph; and so find they in their scriptures, and in their chronicles. On the other part, if they were sepultures, they should not be void within, ne they should have no gates for to enter within; for ye may well know that tombs and sepultures be not made

---

[1] *Pilgrimage*, edited by M. Letts (Hakluyt Society, 1946), p. 127.

[2] Breydenbach, who was there in October 1483, has a delightful description. I have used the German edition of 1486 (without pagination).

of such greatness, nor of such highness; wherefore it is not to believe that they be tombs or sepultures.

Chapter VIII, describing the way to Mount Sinai is from Boldensele, but the statement, 'no man may go on horseback, because that there ne is neither meat for horse ne water to drink' is a direct contradiction of Boldensele, who prides himself on having ridden to Mount Sinai on horseback, although he had camels with him to carry food and water.

In chapter IX we have more about the habits of the Bedouins, and another personal statement: 'And they have often-times war with the sultan and namely that time that I was with him.' At Hebron were the graves of the Patriarchs and their wives, and close by was the cave in the rock where Adam and Eve lived when they were driven out of Paradise, 'and there got they their children,' to which the interesting information is added that Adam was driven out of Paradise on the very day that he was put in, having sinned at once. In the Vale of Mamre was Abraham's tree, called Dirpe or the Dry Tree, which had been there since the beginning of the world. At one time it was green and had leaves, but it died on the day of the Crucifixion. Only when a prince of the world should recover the Holy Land and sing mass under it, would the tree turn green again and bear fruit and leaves. The first part of the story (but not the prophecy) comes from a book on the Holy Land attributed to Odoric, but the Dry Tree has a literature of its own, and deserves a special note. From other sources we learn that, in the time of Constantine, Jews, Christians and heathen all gathered under the Dry Tree for their religious services, and that the Emperor was forced to build a Christian church there to prevent the spot being profaned. Nevertheless, thousands of heathen, Jews and Christians continued to resort there until the place became a kind of fair-ground. Josephus speaks of an oak by which Abraham dwelt and which had stood since the beginning of the world.

47

The first pilgrim apparently to mention the tree was Arculf (A.D.670). He found a church on the spot and a dry trunk, but it had been chipped and cut on all sides on account of the veneration in which it was held. Friar Anselm (1509) describes the tree, which was five or six furlongs from Hebron, as greatly venerated by the Arabs, who covered its branches with pieces of fluttering rags and believed that whoever took even a twig would die within a year. The subsequent history of the tree is difficult to follow. Marco Polo places it in Persia, so does Clavijo (1403–6). It finds a place in the legends associated with the Emperor Frederick II *Stupor Mundi*, who is said to have vanished from the sight of men while wearing a stone of invisibility sent to him by Prester John. The common people refused to believe that the Emperor was dead, and it was Frederick, according to popular belief, who was to fulfil the prophecy and lay down his sceptre beneath the Dry Tree. There is no reason to believe that the story was confined to Germany, and Mandeville may well have heard of it in Liége and tacked it on to his extract from Odoric.[1] He also adds the interesting information that, if a man carried a piece of the tree with him, 'it healeth him from the falling evil, and his horse shall not be a-foundered,' but this comes from Vincent of Beauvais.[2]

The author is now approaching Jerusalem. He describes the Holy Places at Bethlehem, and gives a charming account of how roses first came into the world, the source of which has not been traced. A maiden was accused of fornication and sent to the stake. As the fire began to burn she prayed to our Lord that he would cause her innocence to be known to all men. 'And . . . anon was the fire quenched and out, and the brands that were burning became red rose-trees, and the brands that were not kindled became white rose-trees, full of roses. And these were the first rose-trees

---

[1] See my article in *Notes and Queries*, 191, p. 7 (July 13, 1946).
[2] *Spec. Hist.* XXXI, ch. 59.

and roses, both white and red, that ever any man saw; and thus was this maiden saved by the grace of God.'

Chapters x to xiv deal with Jerusalem and the Holy Places, but these chapters, except where Mandeville relies on Boldensele, are based on earlier descriptions, and there is little to show that the author wrote as an eye-witness. One example may be given. Mandeville claims to have entered the Temple at Jerusalem and gives the dimensions. He then goes on: 'And in the middle place of the temple be many high stages, of fourteen degrees of height, made with good pillars all about; and this place the Jews call *Sancta Sanctorum*, that is to say "Holy of Hallows." ' If by 'stages' ('stage' in the Egerton version) the author means the marble casing of the Holy Rock, he is wrong by about two centuries, for the casing was removed by Saladin in 1187, and the rock again exposed.[1] Chapter xiv contains also a reference to the river called Sabatory, which ran all the days of the week except Saturday, when it rested, a story which has many variants, and is usually associated with the Ten Tribes who were helplessly confined behind it, because they could not cross it on their Sabbath. Later legends transferred the river to the country of Prester John, where we shall meet it again, but it is interesting to note that there is a river near Arka, where Mandeville places the Sabatory river, which still flows intermittently, sometimes flowing two or three times a week, and sometimes not for twenty or thirty days.[2]

Chapter xv contains an account of the Saracens and their law, a chapter which much impressed Yule, but which is now shown to have been taken, with details of the life of Mahomet, from William of Tripoli's *Tractatus de Statu Saracenorum* (c. 1270) and Vincent of Beauvais.[3] This chapter contains the interesting colloquy with the sultan which

---

[1] A later traveller, von Harff (1496–99), speaks of the rock as enclosed with an iron railing. *Pilgrimage*, Hakluyt Society (1946), p. 209.
[2] Warner, p. 191 and authorities there quoted.   [3] *Spec. Hist.* XXIII, ch. 39–67.

Dr. Bovenschen accepts as genuine, but which Sir George Warner regards as fiction, being merely a device of the author to magnify himself and convey a homily of his own on the corruption of the age. As a matter of fact the colloquy bears a strange and suspicious resemblance to the dialogue in Caesarius of Heisterbach (1220–35)[1] between Canon William of Utrecht, when a young man, and a Saracen nobleman after the capture of Acre by Saladin in 1187, which was overlooked by both Bovenschen and Warner. Mandeville has already described in chapter VI how the Sultan gave audience, and has told us about his safe-conduct (chapter XI) sealed with the Sultan's seal, to which great reverence was shown, all lords and common people kneeling down before it, putting it on their heads and kissing it (from Boldensele). He now continues as follows: 'And, therefore, I shall tell you what the soldan told me upon a day in his chamber. He let void out of his chamber all manner of men, lords and others, for he would speak with me in counsel. And there he asked me how the Christian men governed them in our country. And I said him, 'Right well, thanked be to God.' But the Sultan answered:

> Truly Nay! For ye Christian men ne reck right nought, how untruly to serve God! Ye should give ensample to the lewd people for to do well, and ye give them ensample to do evil. For the commons upon festival days, when they should go to church to serve God, then go they to taverns, and be there in gluttony all the day and all night, and eat and drink as beasts that have no reason, and wit not when they have enough. And also the Christian men enforce themselves in all manners that they may, for to fight and for to deceive that one that other. And therewithal they be so proud that they know not how to be clothed, now long, now short, now strait, now large, now sworded, now daggered, and in all manner guises. They should be simple, meek and true, and full of alms-deeds, as Jesu was, in whom they trow, but they be all the contrary, and ever inclined to

---

[1] *Dialogus Miraculorum*, ed. J. Strange, 1851, Bk. IV, cap. xv, translated by Scott and Bland, 1929, I, p. 211, and see "Le Prétendu Séjour de Mandeville en Egypte," by Prof. Chauvin in *Wallonia*, 1902, p. 237.

the evil, and to do evil. And they be so covetous that, for a little silver, they sell their daughters, their sisters and their own wives to put them to lechery. And one withdraweth the wife of another, and none of them holdeth faith to another, but they defoul their law that Christ Jesu betook them to keep for their salvation. And thus, for their sins, have they lost all this land that we hold . . . And that know we well by our prophecies, that Christian men shall win again this land out of our hands, when they serve God more devoutly, but as long as they be of foul and of unclean living (as they be now) we have no dread of them in no kind, for their God will not help them in no wise.

Mandeville tells us that he asked the Sultan how he knew so much about the Christian world, and the reply was that he knew all the state of all the courts of Christian kings and princes and commons 'by his messengers that he sent to all lands, in manner as they were merchants of precious stones, of cloths of gold and of other things, for to know the manner of every country amongst Christian men.' Then the Sultan summoned four of his lords who, to Mandeville's surprise, spoke French as well as he did, as did also the Sultan himself.

Now for Caesarius of Heisterbach. 'Tell me, O youth, how the Christians keep the law of Christ in your country.' He (Canon William), unwilling to tell the actual truth, replied: 'Fairly well.' Then said the admiral [emir]: 'I will tell you the practice of the Christians of this land.' Then follows a very outspoken harangue on the evil habits of Christian men, gluttony, pride, extravagant dress, lechery, the selling of wives and daughters and unclean living, as a result of which the Christians had lost the Holy Land. Mandeville has, as usual, improved on his material, but it is safe to assume that his colloquy with the Sultan never took place.

CHAPTER VI

The Route To Cathay

THE second part of Mandeville's 'Travels' takes us to the Far East, from Trebizond to Ormuz, India, the Indian Archipelago and China. Much, in fact nearly the whole of this, is taken from the travels of Friar Odoric of Pordenone, written in 1330, shortly after his return home.[1] Mandeville never mentions Odoric, except for the oblique reference to two friars minor of Lombardy who accompanied the travellers through the Valley Perilous (see p. 89). One passage, describing the inhabitants of Ormuz sitting in the water up to their necks because of the heat, may come from Marco Polo, but it is the only passage which has been traced to that source, and if Mandeville had taken it from Marco Polo, it is difficult to understand why he did not take much more.

Other sources (as we have seen (p. 31) are Haiton (or Heytoun) the Armenian, and John de Plano Carpini. Haiton supplied Mandeville with his summary description of the countries of Asia and the history of the Mongols. Carpini provided the details of Mongol manners and customs. What version of Odoric Mandeville used is not known, but his debt to it was recognised at a very early date. It was even suggested that Odoric and Mandeville travelled together. Taking these authorities as his ground work, the author inserted any odds and ends of natural history that occurred to him, together with an assortment

---

[1] I have not given references to Odoric, but the passages adapted by Mandeville can easily by found in Yule's *Cathay*, Hakluyt Society, 2nd ed. vol. II, from ch. 16 onwards. With few exceptions, Mandeville follows the same order throughout.

of wonders and marvels to fire the imagination. He then added a number of strange alphabets and such autobiographical details as might be necessary to give an air of verisimilitude to the whole, and as a result we have as entertaining a picture of the East as can be found anywhere. It is interesting to follow Mandeville step by step and see how skilfully he mixed his ingredients, now heightening but never losing control of the marvels he describes, now keeping his tone low, and adding scientific explanations and moral reflections as occasion offered.

In chapter XVI, in Little Armenia, was the castle of the sparrow-hawk kept by an enchantress. Whoever watched the bird for seven days and seven nights, without sleep and without company, could have granted to him his first wish of earthly things. A king of Armenia, a poor man, and a Templar complied with the conditions, but only the poor man chose wisely. He wished for happiness and success in life and obtained riches as well. It is not known where Mandeville found all this, but it seems to go back to the story of the serpent-fairy Melusine, who, with her sisters, was condemned to do penance for their treatment of their father. Other versions mention the king, but the poor man and the Templar seem to be Mandeville's own embellishments. Nor does he tell us where the castle was to be found — 'he that will see such marvels, him behoves some time thus wend out of the way' (Egerton).

Not far from Erzerum was the hill called Ararat on which, in clear weather, men could see the Ark which had come to rest on the mountaintop. It was said that men had reached the summit and put their fingers into the hole whence the devil flew out when Noah said *Benedicite*,[1] but in fact, if Mandeville is to be believed, only one person ever reached the Ark, a monk, and that was due to divine intervention.

---

[1] I have not been able to trace this reference, but the Devil was certainly a passenger. He entered holding on to the tail of an ass, but how he escaped is a mystery. See Baring-Gould, *Legends of O.T. Characters* (1871), I, p. 112.

Velser's German version has a fine picture of Mount Ararat with the Ark perched on the top and the monk climbing up to it. The story has many variants and is as old as Josephus[1] who reports that the Ark still existed in his day and that pieces of the pitch were used as armlets. Mandeville did not take the story from Odoric, who states only that he wished to make the ascent if his companions would have waited for him. Also that the country-folk told him that no one had ascended the mountain, as it did not seem to be the pleasure of the Most High. Haiton[2] tells us that it was not possible to ascend the mountain on account of the snows, but that a black object was to be seen there which was said to be Noah's Ark, but Mandeville probably used Vincent of Beauvais,[3] who does not however refer to the story of the monk. The story that the monk brought down a piece of the Ark and built a monastery at the foot of the mountain, where it was worshipped as a holy relic, comes from Wm. de Rubruck. The relic was seen by the German, Friedrich Parrot, who first climbed Ararat in 1829, but the monastery was destroyed in the earthquake of 1840 and not a soul survived.[4]

Passing beyond the Tower of Babel, we reach the land of Chaldea (chapter XVII), where the men were fair and arrayed in cloth of gold, while the women were right foul and hideous, and are transported, without rhyme or reason, to the land of the Amazons. The story of the Amazons is so old and widespread that it is useless to look for Mandeville's sources, but practically all that Mandeville relates about the Amazons, and much more, is to be found in the forged Letter of Prester John with which Mandeville was certainly familiar. Mandeville's account is as follows:

Beside the land of Chaldea is the land of Amazonia, that is the land of Feminye. And in that realm is all women and no man; not, as some men say, that men may not live there, but for because that the

[1] *Antiq.* XX, II, 2.1; III, 6.   [2] Book I, ch. IX.   [3] *Spec. Nat.* VI, ch. 21.
[4] See my article in *Notes and Queries*, 191, p. 140, 5 Oct. 1946.

women will not suffer no men amongst them to be their sovereigns. For sometime there was a king in that country. And men married as in other countries. And so befell that the king had war with them of Scythia, the which king hight Colopeus, that was slain in battle, and all the good blood of his realm. And when the queen and all the other noble ladies saw that they were all widows, and that all the royal blood was lost, they armed them and as creatures out of wit, they slew all the men of the country that were left; for they would that all the women were widows as the queen and they were. And from that time hitherwards they never would suffer man to dwell amongst them longer than seven days and seven nights ne that no child that were male should dwell amongst them longer than he were nourished and then sent to his father. And when they will have any company of man, then they draw them towards the lands marching next to them. And then they have loves that use them; and they dwell with them an eight days or ten, and then go home again. And if they have any knave child they keep it a certain time, and then send it to the father when he can go alone and eat by himself or else they slay it. And if it be a female they do away that one pap with an hot iron. And if it be a woman of great lineage they do away the left pap that they may the better bear a shield. And if it be woman on foot they do away the right pap, for to shoot with bow turkeys [Turkish bows]; for they shoot well with bows ... This land of Amazonia is an isle, all environed with the sea, save in two places, where be two entries. And beyond that water dwell the men that be their paramours and their loves, where they go to solace them when they will.

On the coast of Chaldea, towards the south, was Ethiopia, where the people were black and lightly drunken. Here we are introduced to the first of Mandeville's fine assortment of monsters, the sciapods, a race of cheerful souls with one foot, which they used, lying on their backs, as a kind of natural umbrella to protect them from the heat of the sun, and whose family tree must be looked for in Pliny and Solinus. We have next a disquisition on diamonds, an interesting passage, if, as has been suggested, the author was himself responsible for a treatise on precious stones. Most of this comes, however, from Pliny, Solinus, Isidore of Seville and Vincent of Beauvais, except the strange statement that diamonds married and had children. 'And they grow together male and female. And they be nourished with the dew of heaven. And they engender commonly and bring forth small children, and multiply and grow all the year. I have often-times assayed that, if a man keep them with a little of the rock and wet them with May-dew, oft-sithes they shall grow every year, and the small will wax great.' I have found no authority for this passage, but it is clear that Mandeville claimed to be an authority on precious stones, and his remarks on the 'gabbers' who go about to sell counterfeit diamonds were obviously intended to be of practical use to lords and knights who sought worship in arms, and who might at any moment have to depend on the magical properties of precious stones to keep them from enchantments and witchcraft, preserve their manhood and give them victory over their enemies, provided, of course, that their cause was just.

India (chapter XVIII) was a strange country, largely composed, if Mandeville is to be believed, of islands. He tells us that there were more than 5,000 habitable islands, without others where no man could dwell, and in these islands were cities and strange creatures more than sufficient to fill any book of marvels to overflowing.

Mandeville always speaks of India as Ind. He divides Ind into three principal parts: Ind the More, a full hot country, Ind the Less, a temperate country, and a third part towards the north, which was cold and frosty. His Ind the More is probably the India we know to-day. His third India would be the country beyond the Himalayas. His Ind the Less is a problem, but it stretched to the land of Media, and is probably the India Minor (or Middle India) of early geographers, which comprised a vast undefined coastal region west of the Indus, and included southern Arabia and some part of Ethiopia. No one in his senses would go to Mandeville for correct geographical information, but this note and reference to the map may serve to show the confusion which existed in men's minds at that time at the mere mention of India.

Odoric is here utilised to the full. The friar's mention of ships without iron in them — the stitched ships of Odoric and Marco Polo — starts Mandeville off on a description of the loadstone rocks and the magnetic sea, to which he returns in chapter xxx, when dealing with the coast of Prester John's country. In the isle of Chana were rats as large as dogs, and the island of Lomb was famous for its pepper forests. Mandeville's account of the pepper forests, and the method of drying the pepper when gathered, is taken largely from Odoric, with additions from Pliny, Isidore, Albertus Magnus, and Jacques de Vitry. Odoric tells us that in the forest were many evil serpents, which had to be burnt out before the pepper could be gathered. Having incorporated all this into his narrative, it seems to have struck Mandeville, who for all his weakness for marvels was a practical person, that if the serpents were burnt, the pepper would be burnt as well. He, therefore, adds the following observation: 'But save their grace of all that say so (Egerton: 'But save their grace, it is not so'), for if they burnt about the trees that bear, the pepper should be burnt, and it would dry up all the virtue, as of any other thing; and then they did themselves much harm, and they should never quench the fire' — an aside which passed almost verbatim into the narrative of a late fifteenth-century traveller, von Harff,[1] and incidentally provided conclusive evidence that von Harff lifted many of his stories straight out of Mandeville, just as Mandeville lifted his from Odoric. There is no doubt, I think, that Mandeville was using Odoric here, but he must also have had beside him the forged Letter of Prester John, for Prester John supplies some of the details not to be found in Odoric. Prester John relates the story as follows: 'And when the pepper is ripe all the people come from the country round about, bringing

---

[1] *Pilgrimage*, Hakluyt Society (1946), p. 170.

with them chaff, straw and very dry timber, with which they surround the whole wood and, when the wind blows strongly, they light fire inside and outside the wood lest any serpent should be able to get out, and so all the serpents perish in the fire which burns very fiercely, except only those which go to shelter in their caves. And behold, when the fire has burnt itself out, men and women, great and small, enter the wood, carrying forks in their hands, and throw out the roasted serpents from the wood with their forks, and make great heaps of them, like grain winnowed from the chaff in a threshing floor.'[1] Then follows an account of certain health-giving salves which were made from the roasted serpents, and which were apt for sterile women. Mandeville tells the story differently. He says that the people anointed their hands and feet with the juice of snails, which frightened the serpents away, but that he was copying and adapting from Prester John's Letter is, I think, beyond doubt.

Not far from the pepper country was the well or fountain of youth. 'Whoso drinketh three times fasting of that water of that well, he is whole of all manner sickness that he hath. And they that dwell there, and drink often of that well, they never have sickness; and they seem always young.' This comes, again, from Prester John's Letter. After describing certain people who ate celestial bread and lived for 500 years the Letter continues: 'However, at the end of 100 years they grow young again, and are renewed by drinking thrice of a certain fountain which issues forth from the root of a certain tree there, to wit in the said island. And this water, thus three times consumed or drunk, then, as I say, they throw off their age of 100 years and are thus relieved of it, so that without delay they appear to be of the age of thirty or forty years and no more. And so each 100 years they are rejuvenated and are altogether changed.'[2] We have here an excellent example of how Mandeville made

[1] Zarncke, *Der Priester Johannes*, p. 912.
[2] Zarncke, p. 913 (interpolation E3).

use of his material. He avoids the difficulty of having to introduce and explain the rejuvenated centenarians, and of endowing himself with immortality by deliberately writing down the story and adding: 'I have drunken thereof three or four sithes, and yet, methinketh I fare the better,' and he hopes to do so 'until the time that God of his grace will make me to pass out this deadly life' (Egerton).

Chapter XIX starts off with a description of the church of St. Thomas at Mabaron and of the judgments pronounced by the saint's hand. The arm was preserved in a vessel outside the tomb — some pictures show a ghostly hand protruding from the tomb itself — and, if two parties went to law, they put their bills, or statements of their case, into the outstretched hand. Thereupon the saint cast away the false bill and retained the true one. This story is not in Odoric and is not found in precisely the same form elsewhere. Nor does the story come from Prester John's Letter. We are told, however, in one of the documents associated with the Letter that the saint's body was preserved intact, and that, on the Apostle's feast day, the holy body was placed in a pontifical chair close to the altar. When the time came to administer the eucharist, the wafers were placed in the saint's right hand, but if a heretic or a sinner drew near to communicate, forthwith, in the sight of all, the Apostle withdrew his hand and closed it, whereupon the heretic or sinner either repented and in penitence received the sacrament or died.[1] That the story as related in this document was well known to, and doubted by, at least one Mandeville translator in the fifteenth century appears from the Latin edition of Mandeville printed by Gerard Leeu at Antwerp (Gouda) 1485. Here the translator, at the end of chapter XXVIII, refers to the story of the administration of the sacrament, but describes it as a vulgar fable, adding the following cryptic note: *sed non est ita, et nunquam fuit.*

[1] See generally my article in *Notes and Queries*, 188, p. 179 (May 5, 1945) and 'Transactions of the Royal Hist. Society,' 4th Series, XXIX, 1947, pp. 19–26.

The church where St. Thomas lay was full of great idols, of which the smallest was as big as two men. The chief idol was seated and was covered with gold and precious stones. This idol was a great object of worship, and the people went on pilgrimage to it, cutting their legs and arms with sharp knives, sprinkling their blood on the idol, and even sacrificing their children to it. Then follows a description of the juggernaut car, a remarkable and gruesome piece of descriptive writing which is worth quoting in full.

And ye shall understand that when there be great feasts and solemnities of that idol, as the dedication of the church and the throning of the idol, all the country about meet there together. And they set this idol upon a car with great reverence, well arrayed with cloths of gold, of rich cloths of Tartary, of Camaka, and other precious cloths. And they lead him about the city with great solemnity. And before the car go first in procession all the maidens of the country, two and two together full ordinatly. And after these maidens go the pilgrims. And some of them fall down under the wheels of the car, and let the car go over them, so that they be dead anon. And some have their arms or their limbs all to-broken, and some the sides. And all this do they for love of their god, in great devotion. And them thinketh that the more pain, and the more tribulation that they suffer for love of their god, the more joy they shall have in another world. And, shortly to say you, they suffer so great pains, and so hard martyrdoms for love of their idol, that a Christian man, I trow, durst not take upon him the tenth part the pain for love of our Lord Jesu Christ. And after, I say you, before the car go all the minstrels of the country without number, with diverse instruments, and they make all the melody they can.

Odoric adds that not a year passed without 500 persons perishing in this manner, their bodies being burnt as those of holy men who had killed themselves for their god.

In chapter xxi we have a description of the island of Java, 'nigh two thousand mile in circuit,' which is taken almost literally from Odoric, although he says that the island had a compass of 3,000 miles. The king had a marvellous palace, richer than any in the world. The steps and the pavements of the halls and chambers were of choice gold and silver, and on the walls were pictures of knights in battle, the crowns and the circles about their heads being made of precious stones and pearls, 'so that no man would trow the riches of that palace but he had seen it.' The King of Java was so powerful that he had often overthrown the Great Chan of Cathay, who was jealous of his country and riches, but neither Mandeville nor Odoric gives details of these wars, and Marco Polo is equally vague. We are now reaching the land of golden palaces, and there is nothing improbable in the description of the palace at Java when one remembers that gold leaf glitters as much as gold plate.

In the adjoining island of Pathen were trees bearing meal, honey and venom, against which there was no antidote but one, a concoction of leaves stamped down and tempered with water. Here Mandeville differs from Odoric who states that the antidote is *stercus humanum* diluted with water, and Mandeville adds a note of his own, the source of which has not been traced: 'Of this venom the Jews had let seek of one of their friends for to empoison all Christianity, as I have heard them say in their confession before their dying, but thanked be Almighty God they failed of their purpose' — a reference possibly to the very general belief in the fourteenth century that the Jews were responsible for the Black Death. The giant bamboos in the same island come from Odoric, but the rattans, of which Mandeville claims to have seen huge specimens on the sea-shore, twenty of his fellows being unable to lift or carry one away, have a stranger and more ancient ancestry. They are described almost in identical terms in the spurious Letter of Alexander the Great to Aristotle on the marvels of India.

We come now to the isle of Calonak (possibly Champa, part of South Cochin China), a fair land and well supplied with goods. The King had 14,000 elephants or more, and a prodigious family. 'And the king of that country hath as many wives as he will. For he maketh search all the country to get him the fairest maidens that may be found, and maketh them to be brought before him. And he taketh one one night, and another another night, and so forth continually suing; so that he hath a thousand wives or more. And he lieth never but one night with one of them, and another night with another; but if that one happen to be more lusty to his pleasance than another. And therefore the king getteth full many children, sometime an hundred, sometime a two-hundred and sometime more.'

In the isle of Calonak was another great marvel, for here the fish cast themselves on the land in such numbers that a man could see nothing but fish. After three days those that survived withdrew into the sea, and others took their places. No man knew the cause, but the people of the country said that it was to do reverence to their king, who had so many children that God sent the fish to do him homage, and to supply him and his people with food. This is from Odoric, and the story is told more briefly by Marco Polo. Warner adds a note referring to Guillemard's *Cruise of the Marchesa*, 1886, where it is stated that much the same kind of thing could be seen in the Avatcha river, which runs into Avatcha Bay in South Kamtchatka. Here the traveller saw hundreds of fish absolutely touching one another, so that the horses nearly trod on them. On enquiry he found the phenomenon was an annual one, of as constant occurrence as the breaking up of the ice. The story may also have something to do with the vast shoals of sardines frequenting the coast of Ceylon.

Mandeville now introduces us to a whole family of human monsters in the islands of Tracoda, Nacumera, Silha (Ceylon) and elsewhere. These include troglodytes, who ate the flesh of serpents and hissed as serpents do, dog-headed men and women, a collection of one-eyed giants, men 'whose heads do grow beneath their shoulders,' flat-faced people, men with a lip so large that they wrapped themselves round with it like a cloak when they lay in the sun,[1] dwarfs with a round hole in place of a mouth, through which they sucked their food and drink with the aid of a pipe or tube, men with ears hanging down to their knees, people with horses feet, others who went on all fours, hermaphrodites, and men who crawled on their knees. It is needless to say that we shall look in vain for these creatures in Odoric, although Ramusio's second Italian text[2] speaks of horses with six legs, ostriches with two heads, pigmies, a one-eyed giant, and a pair of creatures, male and female, a span high, with big heads and long legs who fed themselves with the foot. Mandeville's monsters, or most of them, come from Pliny, Solinus, and Isidore of Seville, by way of Vincent of Beauvais, and provided a magnificent opportunity for Mandeville's illustrators, of which they took full advantage.

[1] Compare the African custom of enlarging the lower lip with a series of progressively larger wooden plates.
[2] Yule, in *Cathay and the Way Thither*. Hakluyt Society, 2nd ed. II, p. 229.

CHAPTER VII

Cathay and the Great Chan

A PPROACHING Cathay and the court of the Great Chan, we are now to my mind among the most inter-esting chapters in the book. Mandeville relies mainly on Odoric, Haiton and Carpini, but the various narratives are dovetailed together with great skill and exhibit Mande-ville at his best.

He first takes his readers to the city of Latorin (Canton), which was larger than Paris and well supplied with ships and creatures of all kinds, including geese with red necks and cock's combs (the Guinea goose) and a profusion of serpents which the people regarded as a great delicacy. The country thereabouts was well supplied with food and wine, and among the strange creatures were hens without feathers, which bore wool like sheep (the silk-fowl, or *gallus lanatus*, of Odoric).[1] The traveller now reaches Cassay (Hang-Chow), which he calls the City of Heaven. So does Odoric. It was fifty miles about and strongly inhabited, so that in one house men had ten households. Odoric has 100 miles in compass and ten or twelve households in a tene-ment. There were twelve gates (Odoric agrees). It sat on a lake like Venice (Odoric 'like the City of Venice.') There were 12,000 bridges with strong towers, in which dwelt the wardens. (Odoric has 12,000, on each of which were stationed guards). A good wine grew there 'that men clepe Bigon, that is full mighty and gentle in drinking.' Odoric has Bigni, reputed a noble drink. Then comes the curious description of the garden of transmigrated souls in an abbey

[1] See Odoric in Yule's *Cathay and the Way Thither*, 2nd ed, ch. 29 ff.

of monks near Cassay. In this garden were divers beasts, apes, marmosets and baboons, which assembled after dinner to eat the fragments left over from the meal. This is worked up almost literally from Odoric, who says that the beasts numbered 3,000 and had faces like men. Mandeville tells us that the beasts that were fair were the souls of worthy men, and they that were foul were the souls of poor men of rude commons. We now have another instance of Mandeville's skill in introducing those little personal touches which give the impression of individual experience. 'And I asked them,' he says, 'if it had not been better to have given that relief to poor men, rather than to those beasts. And they answered me and said, that they had no poor men amongst them in that country; and though it had been so that poor men had been among them, yet were it greater alms to give it to those souls that do there their penance.' This might be interpreted as something of a snub, but it certainly makes the story live.

On the way to Chilenfo (Nan-king) Mandeville crosses a great river called Dalay (Odoric, Talay). Both agree that it was the greatest river in the world. The river passed through the land of pigmies. Here Mandeville relies on Odoric and other sources, including, of course, Vincent of Beauvais, but his statement that the pigmies married and had children at six months must be a record. Odoric says that the women married in their fifth year.

The city of Cambelech (Peking) is described at length from Odoric. With the new city of Caydo (Taydo in Odoric) built by Kublai, in 1267, it had a circuit of twenty (Odoric says forty) miles. Mandeville's description of the hall of the palace is mainly from Odoric, but some passages are worth quoting, if only for the glimpse they give us of the mysterious and splendid East.

> The palace, where his siege is, is both great and passing fair. And within the palace, in the hall, there be twenty-four pillars of fine gold. And all the walls be covered within of red skins of beasts that men

clepe panthers, that be fair beasts and well smelling, so that for the sweet odour of those skins no evil air may enter into the palace. Those skins be as red as blood, and they shine so bright against the sun, that unnethe no man may behold them. And many folk worship those beasts, when they meet them first at morning, for their great virtue and for the good smell that they have. And those skins they prize more than though they were plate of fine gold.'

This is mainly adapted from Odoric, but from what source Mandeville got his panthers is not known, (Odoric speaks only of 'skins of red leather, said to be the finest in the world') unless they come from Vincent of Beauvais, who has *panthera . . . rugitum magnum emittet cum odore suavissimo quasi omnium aromatum*[1] Mandeville then continues:

And the hall of the palace is full nobly arrayed, and full marvellously attired on all parts in all things that men apparel with any hall. And first, at the chief of the hall is the emperor's throne, full high, where he sitteth at the meat. And that is of fine precious stones, bordered all about with pured gold and precious stones, and great pearls. And the grees [steps] that he goeth up to the table be of precious stones mingled with gold.

And at the left side of the emperor's siege is the siege of his first wife, one degree lower than the emperor; and it is of jasper, bordered with gold and precious stones. And the siege of his second wife is also another siege, more lower than his first wife; and it is also of jasper, bordered with gold, as that other is. And the siege of the third wife is also more low, by a degree, than the second wife. For he hath always three wives with him, where that ever he be . . . And after at the right side of the emperor first sitteth his eldest son that shall reign after him. And he sitteth also one degree lower than the emperor, in such manner of sieges as do the empresses. And after him sit other great lords of his lineage, every of them a degree lower than the other, as they be of estate. And the emperor hath his table alone by himself, that is of gold and of precious stones, or of crystal bordered with gold, and full of precious stones or of amethysts, or of lignum aloes that cometh out of paradise, or of ivory bound or bordered with gold. And every one of his wives hath also her table by herself. And his eldest son and the other lords also, and the ladies, and all that sit with the emperor have tables alone by

[1] *Spec. Nat.* XIX. chap. 99.

themselves, full rich. And there ne is no table but that it is worth an huge treasure of goods.

And under the emperor's table sit four clerks that write all that the emperor saith, be it good, be it evil; for all that he saith must be holden, for he may not change his word, ne revoke it.

In the midst of the hall was what the Cotton version calls a 'mountour' ('ascensory' in the Egerton version) which seems to be a mistranslation of Odoric's pigna (jar). It was a great reservoir of drink, wrought of gold and precious stones. Under the 'mountour' were conduits with vessels of gold, so that the guests might drink their fill. Odoric tells us that the jar was made of a certain precious stone called *Merdacas* (jade), but Mandeville shies at this.

Odoric speaks now of peacocks of gold, which flapped their wings and made as if they would dance, which was done by diabolic art, or by some engine underground. Mandeville copies this, but adds some interesting remarks which might at first sight appear to be his own. He reports of the local astrologers that they were subtle men, for malice and farcasting, surpassing all men under heaven. They claimed to see with two eyes, whereas Christian men who were blind in cunning, saw only with one. This is not in Odoric. It is taken almost literally from Haiton.[1] But what follows is Mandeville's own. 'I did great business for to have learned that craft, but the master told me that he had made a vow to his god to teach it to no creature, but only to his eldest son.'

The state of the Great Chan's court is next described, almost entirely from Odoric. Above the emperor's table was a vine of gold with clusters of grapes made of precious stones, 'so properly made that it seemeth a very vine bearing kindly grapes.' This is not from Odoric: it comes

[1] 'Homines vero illius patrie sunt sagacissimi et omni calliditate repleti et ideo in omni arte et scientia vilipendunt alias nationes et dicunt quod ipsi soli sunt qui duobus oculis respiciunt, Latini vero uno lumine tantum vident, sed omnes alias naciones asserunt esse cecas.' Haiton, Bk. I, ch. 1.

straight from the palace of Porus, where it was seen by
Alexander the Great. I close the description of the Great
Chan's court with the following extracts from chapters
XXIII and XXV.

And before the emperor's table stand great lords and rich barons
and other that serve the emperor at the meat. And no man is so
hardy to speak a word, but if the emperor speak to him; but if it be
minstrels that sing songs and tell jests or other disports, to solace
with the emperor. And all the vessels that men be served with in the
hall or in chambers be of precious stones, and specially at great
tables, either of jasper or of crystal or of amethysts or of fine gold.
And the cups be of emeralds and of sapphires, or of topazes, of
perydoz, and of many other precious stones. Vessels of silver is
there none, for they tell no price thereof to make no vessels of: but
they make thereof grecings [steps] and pillars and pavements to halls
and chambers. And before the hall door stand many barons and
knights clean armed to keep that no man enter, but if it be the will
or the commandment of the emperor, or but if they be servants or
minstrels of the household; and other none is not so hardy, to
neighen nigh the hall door . . . And at one side of the emperor's
table sit many philosophers that be proved for wise men in many divers
sciences, as of astronomy, necromancy, geomancy, pyromancy, hydro-
mancy, of augury and of many other sciences . . . And at certain
hours, when them thinketh time, they say to certain officers that
stand before them, ordained for the time to fulfil their command-
ments: Make peace ! And then say the officers, Now peace ! listen !
And after that saith another of the philosophers: Every man do reverence and incline to the emperor, that is God's Son and sovereign
lord of all the world ! For now is the time. And then every man
boweth his head toward the earth. And then commandeth the same
philosopher again: Stand up ! And they do so. And at another hour,
saith another philosopher: Put your little finger in your ears ! And
anon they do so. And at another hour, saith another philosopher:
Put your hand before your mouth ! And anon they do so. And at
another hour saith another philosopher Put your hand upon your
head! And after that he biddeth them to do their hand away. And
they do so.
And so from hour to hour they command certain things; and they
say that those things have diverse significations. And I asked them
privily what those things betokened. And one of the masters told
me that the bowing of the head at that hour betokened this: that

all those that bowed their heads should evermore after be obeissant and true to the emperor, and never, for gifts ne for promise in no kind, to be false ne traitor unto him for good nor evil. And the putting of the little finger in the ear betokeneth, as they say, that none of them ne shall not hear speak no contrarious thing to the emperor but that he shall tell it anon to his council or discover it to some men that will make relation to the emperor, though he were his father or brother or son. And so forth, of all other things that is done by the philosophers, they told me the causes of many diverse things.

All this, as I have said, comes from Odoric, but it is presented with great skill. The readers' attention is held, partly by the manner in which the various episodes are put together, and partly by the language employed, and that is surely the great art of story-telling. But there was one remark which Mandeville missed. At the end of the list of orders issued by the philosophers, Odoric adds one more: 'Bolt meal,' after which, apparently, the much-harassed courtiers fell upon their food. It is a pity that Mandeville overlooked this. It is true that in another place he tells us (from Carpini) that the Tartars ate hounds, lions, leopards, mares, foals, asses, rats and mice, and that in the isle of Latorin no feast without cooked serpents was a feast at all, but he says little about the food served at the Great Chan's table.

The description of the Summer Palace (chapter XXIII) has not the charm and magic of Coleridge's stately pleasure dome built by Kubla Khan at Xanadu. Indeed, the Summer Palace described by Mandeville (and Odoric) was not at Shandu at all, which was some days' journey from Peking, but within the curtilage of the city palace. It must however have been an enchanting place.

And in the garden of the great palace there is a great hill, upon the which there is another palace; and it is the most fair and the most rich that any man may devise. And all about the palace and the hill be many trees bearing many diverse fruits. And all about that hill be ditches, great and deep, and beside them be great vivaries on that one part and on that other. And there is a full fair bridge to pass over the ditches. And in these vivaries be so many wild geese and ganders and wild ducks and swans and herons that is without number. And all about these ditches and vivaries is the great garden full of wild beasts. So that when the great Chan will have any disport on that, to take any of the wild beasts or of the fowls, he will let chase them and take them at the windows without going out of his chamber.

Next follows a description of Tartar table habits ('all the commons there eat without cloth upon their knees, and they eat all manner of flesh and little of bread, and after meat they wipe their hands upon their skirts') which is taken not from Odoric, but probably from Carpini, by way of Vincent of Beauvais.[1] Then comes the following statement, which is remarkable for its brevity rather than its truth, for the author was not a man to waste words: 'And ye shall understand that my fellows and I with our yeomen, we served the emperor, and were his soldiers fifteen months against the King of Mancy' (who incidentally was dead long before Mandeville claimed to have fought against him.) In fact, of course, there is not a scrap of evidence to show that Mandeville was ever in or near China.

Chapter xxiv ('Wherefore he is called the Great Chan') is taken almost literally from Haiton, Book III, except that the description of the emperor's seal is dovetailed in from Carpini. Nearly the whole of chapter xxv on the Great Chan's court is supplied by Odoric, but the effect is heightened by the introduction of fresh marvels, for which there is no authority except in Mandeville's fertile imagination:

And then come jugglers and enchanters that do many marvels; for they make to come in the air, by seeming, the sun and the moon to every man's sight. And after they make the night so dark that no man may see nothing. And after they make the day to come again, fair and pleasant with bright sun, to every man's sight. And then they bring in dances of the fairest damsels of the world and richest

[1] *Spec. Hist.* XXIX, ch. 78.

arrayed. And after they make to come in other damsels bringing cups of gold full of milk of diverse beasts, and give drink to lords and to ladies. And then they make knights to joust in arms full lustily; and they run together a great random, and they frussch together full fiercely, and they break their spears so rudely that the truncheons fly in sprouts and pieces all about the hall. And then they make to come in hunting for the hart and for the boar, with hounds running with open mouth. And many other things they do by craft of their enchantments, that it is a marvel for to see.

The effect of magic is heightened in the Egerton version, where it is made clear that the knights jousted 'in the air, well armed,' but the only justification for all this in Odoric is the statement that jugglers caused cups of gold full of good wine to fly through the air and offer themselves to the lips of all who wished to drink it, a very ancient piece of Eastern jugglery noted by Marco Polo nearly a hundred years earlier.

Chapter xxv also contains an interesting note on Chinese currency :

> The emperor may dispend as much as he will without estimation; for he not dispendeth ne maketh no money but of leather imprinted, or of paper. And of that money is some of greater price and some of less price, after the diversity of his statutes. And when that money hath run so long that it beginneth to waste, then men bear it to the emperor's treasury and then they take new money for the old. And that money goeth throughout all the country and throughout all his provinces, for there and beyond them they make no money neither of gold nor of silver; and therefore he may dispend enough, and outrageously. And of gold and silver that men bear in his country he makes cylours (canopies), pillars and pavements in his palace, and other diverse things, what him liketh.

It was thought at one time that Mandeville was an independent authority for this, but, in fact, except for the statement that the money was printed on leather, it is all in Odoric or Marco Polo.

The emperor's postal service was not as remarkable as that in use in Prester John's country, where the letters were delivered by flying dragons, but it was effective enough. The following is, as usual, from Odoric.

> And there is a marvellous custom in that country (but it is profitable), that if any contarious thing that should be prejudice or grievance to the emperor in any kind, anon the emperor hath tidings thereof and full knowledge in a day, though it be three or four journeys from him or more. For his ambassadors take their dromedaries or their horses, and they prick in all that ever they may toward one of the inns. And when they come there, anon they blow an horn. And anon they of the inn know well enough that there be tidings to warn the emperor of some rebellion against him. And then anon they make other men ready, in all haste that they may, to bear letters and prick in all that ever they may, till they come to the other inns with their letters. And then they make fresh men ready to prick forth with the letters toward the emperor, while that the last bringer rest him, and bait his dromedary or his horse. And so, from inn to inn, till it come to the emperor. And thus anon hath he hasty tidings of anything that beareth charge, by his couriers, that run so hastily throughout all country. And also when the emperor sendeth his couriers hastily throughout his land, every one of them hath a large thong full of small bells, and when they neigh near to the inns of other couriers that be also ordained by the journeys, they ring their bells, and anon the other couriers make them ready, and run their way unto another inn. And thus runneth one to other, full speedily and swiftly, till the emperor's intent be served in all haste. And these couriers be clept *Chydydo*, after their language, that is to say, a messenger.

It would be interesting to identify Mandeville's Great Chan, but it is impossible to be certain. He tells us that when he was there: 'their emperor had to name Thiaut, so that he was clept Thiaut-Chan,' and he then gives the names of his sons and wives, but he is merely giving, as contemporaries of his own, the list of the sons and grandsons of Jenghis Khan, supplied a century before by Carpini.[1] The Chan that Mandeville describes was not a Christian potentate,

[1] Vincent (*Spec. Hist.* XXXI, ch. 13), gives the list of Jenghis Kkan's sons and grandsons. Mandeville's Thiaut is probably Carpini's Cuyne (Kuyuk), whose coronation he attended, as quoted in Vincent, *Spec. Hist.* XXXI, ch. 31. Vincent also calls him Cuinae.

but he suffered Christians to dwell in his lordship and was in fact the greatest and most tolerant ruler on earth.

'Under the firmament is not so great a lord, ne so mighty, ne so rich as is the great Chan; not Prester John, that is emperor of the high Ind, ne the Soldan of Babylon, ne the Emperor of Persia. All these ne be not in comparison to the great Chan, neither of might, ne of noblesse, ne of royalty, ne of riches; for in all these he passeth all earthly princes. Wherefore it is great harm that he believeth not faithfully in God. And natheles he will gladly hear speak of God. And he suffereth well that Christian men dwell in his lordship, and that men of his faith be made Christian men, if they will, throughout all his country; for he defendeth no man to hold no law other than him liketh.'

In chapters xxvii and xxviii we have a brief summary of Haiton's account of Asiatic geography, with an entertaining description of the Land of Darkness. The story was that an emperor of Persia set out to destroy all Christian men, but as he was riding against a company of Christians, with intent to slay them, anon a thick cloud came down and covered this cursed emperor and all his host. There they were doomed to live in utter darkness until the Judgment Day, nothing being known of them except that, out of the darkness, people heard voices and the neighing of horses and the crowing of cocks. Haiton tells us that he had seen this marvel himself,[1] but Mandeville shows unusual restraint in not claiming to have done so. Chapter xxix contains the story of the vegetable lamb, a distorted account of the cotton plant, about which scientists were still disputing in the seventeenth century. 'And there groweth a manner of fruit, as though it were gourds. And when they be ripe, men cut them a-two, and men find within a little beast, in flesh, in bone, and blood, as though it were a little lamb without wool. And men eat

---

[1] 'In regno Georgie apparet quoddam stupendum mirabile et valde monstruosum, quod dicere non auderem, neque credidissem relacione cujusquam nisi propriis occulis aspexissem. Sed quia personaliter ibi fui et fide vidi eciam oculata, dico quod in illis partibus est quedam provincia que vocatur Hanisem . . .' Haiton then continues with the story. Bk. I, ch. x.

both the fruit and the beast. And that is a great marvel.'
This comes with fabulous additions from Odoric, and is
followed, as if to drive home the truth of the story, by the
statement: 'of that fruit I have eaten, although it were
wonderful, but that I know well that God is marvellous in
his works.'

We have now a long account of Gog and Magog and the
enclosed nations shut up behind the Caspian mountains by
Alexander the Great, a legend which may have been taken
from a variety of sources, including J. de Vitry, Vincent
of Beauvais[1] the Alexander romances and Prester John's
Letter. The whole subject has been studied by a learned
American historian, A. R. Anderson, in recent years,[2] and
it is sufficient to say here that Gog and Magog were two
great cannibal nations (to which in due time the Ten Tribes
were added) which Alexander subdued and banished to the
inmost recesses of the Caucasus, where by a miracle of
God (vouchsafed to Alexander, although he was a paynim)
the mountains closed and locked them in on all sides. There
they were to remain until the time of anti-Christ, when they
would break out and destroy the world. This was a story
after Mandeville's own heart and he does full justice to it.
In some versions the enclosed people were kept in subjection and terror by twelve trumpets, so cunningly contrived that they resounded with every breeze. Mandeville
does not mention the trumpets, but he speaks of the iron
gates built by Alexander, and tells us that in the time of
anti-Christ a fox would mine a hole by the gates and pierce
the earth until he came to the imprisoned people, who
would follow and dig themselves out.

Mandeville speaks also of another passage kept by the
Queen of the Amazons (of all people) which led to a desert
where there was no water, and which was full of dragons,

---

[1] *Spec. Hist.* IV, ch. 43.
[2] A. R. Anderson, *Alexander's Gate*, Med. Academy of America, Monograph 5,
Camb. Mass. 1932.

serpents and venemous beasts. Even if it happened that some, by fortune, should find this exit, they would be Jews, and, supposing that they did not die of starvation or fall a prey to the dragons and serpents, they would speak only Hebrew, and no one would understand them. If, as is possible, Mandeville was relying in part on Prester John's Letter, it is strange that he missed one story which would have been greatly to his liking, for it is related there that it was Prester John's pleasure to let the cannibal nations out and lead them against his enemies, whom they devoured until neither man nor beast remained. After this cannibal feast they were driven back to captivity. Chapter xxix ends with a description of the gryphon, or giant rukh of Marco Polo and the 'Arabian Nights,' which was stronger than eight lions and a hundred eagles, and which could carry off in its talons a great horse, or two oxen yoked together as they went to plough. 'For he hath his talons so long and so large and great upon his feet, as though they were horns of great oxen or of bugles or of kine, so that men make cups of them to drink of. And of their ribs and of the pens of their wings, men make bows, full strong, to shoot with arrows and quarrels.'[1] But we are now approaching the land of Prester John, called the isle of Pentexoire, where we shall find even greater marvels than in the fabled country of Cathay.

---

[1] The horns of all kinds of animals serving as drinking cups or reliquaries were described as gryphons' claws in the Middle Ages. There is a curved ibex horn at the British Museum which was catalogued among the treasures of Durham in the fourteenth century as a gryphon's talon sacred to St. Cuthbert. British Museum, *Guide to Medieval Antiquities* (1924), p. 110.

CHAPTER VIII

Prester John

CHAPTER XXX describes the country of Prester John, which we are told was an island, but there was nothing strange in this, as Mandeville speaks of India, Cathay and Tibet as islands. Mandeville did not think as much of Prester John as he did of the Great Chan, but he adds a personal statement (in the Egerton version) that he and his fellows saw all these wonders, having dwelt at Prester John's court for a long time, and it was Mandeville who first introduced the famous Letter to English readers.

It is difficult for us to realise to-day the spell which this legendary Christian priest-king cast over men's minds in the Middle Ages. The story penetrated into every country. The forged Letter of Prester John was translated into practically every European language. There are versions in Anglo-Norman, in the Scots dialect, in Gaelic and even in Hebrew. Professor Zarncke, who established the text of the Letter more than sixty years ago, lists close on a hundred manuscripts, of which ten are in the British Museum. The printed editions of the fifteenth century would require a study to themselves.[1]

The earliest reference to Prester John in Western literature occurs in the Chronicle of Otto of Freising in the year 1145, but the legend of an all-powerful ruler, who is said to have received the rite of baptism, and even ordination, must be much older. It belongs probably to the period of the

---

[1] See my articles in *Notes and Queries*, vol. 188 (1945), pp. 178, 204, 246, vol. 189, p. 4, where all the authorities are collected, also *Transactions* of the Royal Hist. Society, 4th Series, vol. XXIX (1947), p. 19.

introduction of Christianity into Tartary, and was wide-spread in the East before it reached Europe.

Some twenty years later than the date mentioned by Otto of Freising, that is about 1165, began the circulation of the famous Letter which, in Gibbon's words, long amused the credulity of Europe and was subsequently to evaporate in a monstrous fable. The Letter purports to be addressed by Prester John to the Emperor Manuel and relates in extravagant terms, and in great detail, the marvels of the Prester's kingdom and the extent of his dominions. At this time Europe was thoroughly alarmed at the increasing power of the infidel, and the idea of a Christian potentate, whose territory extended over the three Indias, to the sun-rising and back again to the Tower of Babel, who was fabulously rich, as well as endowed with miraculous powers, and who was prepared to march to the assistance of the Crusaders, was irresistible. It filled the early maps with monsters and fables, gave a new impetus to geographical discovery, brought fresh hope to Christendom, and provided story-tellers with material which lasted for centuries.

The manuscripts of the Letter fall into six groups, one containing the uninterpolated text, the remaining five being distinguished by a series of interpolations which grew up as additions to the text from time to time. As the Letter passed from hand to hand and came to be copied and re-copied, fresh and extravagant details were incorporated to meet the growing demand for wonders and marvels, until some of the interpolations are almost as long as the Letter itself, but Mandeville appears to have used the text as a whole, and there is at present no need to go into the vexed questions of how and when the interpolations came into being.[1]

Mandeville follows the Letter with some care, adding at times certain highly-coloured details of his own. Some

[1] The Letter, without the interpolations, has been translated by Sir Denison Ross in *Travel and Travellers of the Middle Ages*, edited by A. P. Newton (1926), p. 174. An abstract of the Letter, with the interpolations, is given in my articles in *Notes and Queries* referred to above.

twenty episodes in Mandeville can be traced to the Letter, and the same order is preserved throughout.

As time went on and no genuine traveller was able to meet with Prester John in Asia, the Asiatic legend faded away, and Prester John was transferred with all his marvels, to Ethiopia, where the Portuguese tried, not very successfully, to locate him. This transfer gave rise to a number of interesting speculations, among others, whether Prester John was black or white, or merely a mulatto of mongrel complexion, a problem to which Sir Thomas Browne devoted an amusing and interesting passage in his *Vulgar Errors*,[1] but Mandeville was content to look for Prester John in Asia, and it is to Prester John's Asiatic kingdom that we must now direct our steps.

The only approach to Prester John's country was by sea, and the voyage was likely to be perilous, for the seas thereabouts were infested with loadstones or magnetic rocks, which lured ships to destruction by drawing out their nails, drowned the sailors and left the hulks to rot. For this reason wise mariners in those parts used stitched ships without a scrap of iron in them and so escaped destruction.[2] Mandeville mentions the loadstone rocks in chapter XVIII. He does not tell us that he sailed the Magnetic Sea, but he claims to have seen the wrecks afar off, the masts and sailyards looking like a great island of trees and brushwood, 'full of thorns and briars, great plenty,' as it were a great wood or grove — an unforgettable picture. Mandeville got the story probably from Vincent of Beauvais,[3] but it was widespread in the Middle Ages. It passed from the East into the European literature of romance and died slowly. The Germans associated it with the Liver or Clotted Sea, in which the water was so 'livered' or thick that it impeded progress. They placed there a magnetic mountain. Attracted by the Magnetic Mountain, ships with iron in them were

[1] Bk. VI, ch. x.   [2] On the stitched ships see Yule's *Marco Polo*, I, p. 117.
[3] *Spec. Nat.* VIII chap. 21.

drawn irresistibly thither, and once in the Liver Sea their fate was sealed and the crew died of starvation, a tradition preserved to modern times by the stories of the Sargasso Sea. That the magnetic rocks were still popular at the end of the fifteenth century is clear from the travels of the German traveller von Harff (1496–99). He claims to have seen them between Aden and Socotra.[1]

Behaim, the geographer (d. 1507), shows the magnetic rocks in his great globe between Java Major and the main-land of India, and the story was still being seriously debated by Sir Thomas Browne as late as 1646. For the rest, the description of Prester John's kingdom comes, but without many of its inconsistencies and extravagances, from the famous Letter, and is in strange conflict with Odoric's sober statement that not one hundredth part of what was related of Prester John was true, and that his principal city was inferior to Vicenza. Prester John was of course a Christian. He had seventy-two provinces under him, and in every province was a king. And these kings had kings under them, and all were tributaries of Prester John. The Letter states that there were no poor in that happy land, and that thieves and liars dared not raise their heads. There was no crime, flattery or strife, but abundance of riches for all. Mandeville compresses these happy virtues into one brief sentence: 'and they set not by no barretts ne by cautels, nor of no deceits.' Then comes a description of the famous Gravelly Sea, which had its origin, no doubt, in the shifting sands of the desert. The sea was all gravel and sand, without water, and the sand moved and swelled like the sea and was never still. It was impossible to cross it, and no man knew what lay beyond. But, although there was no water, 'yet men find therein and on the banks full good fish of other manner of kind and shape than men find in any other sea, and they

---

[1] See my translation of von Harff's *Travels* (Hakluyt Society 1946), p. 156. J. L. Lowes, 'The Dry Sea and the Carrenare,' in *Modern Philology*, III, p. 43 and *Notes and Queries*, vol. 191 (1946), p. 47.

be of right good taste and delicious to man's meat.' The Egerton version adds, 'I John Mandeville ate of them.' Odoric mentions a sea of sand in the Persian desert, but says nothing about the fish.

In Prester John's country was also another marvellous sea which flowed from Paradise, carrying precious stones, wood and sand to the Gravelly Sea, where it disappeared. On three days a week it flowed and no man could cross it, but on the other days it could be crossed. This is an Alexander story, but recalls the Sabbath river of Josephus, to which Mandeville refers in chapter XIV, which flowed all the days of the week except on Saturday, when it rested. In the Letter it is stated that behind this river were the Ten Tribes, and until a crossing could be made on some day other than the Sabbath, the Ten Tribes were hopelessly confined, but Mandeville passes this by.

We have next a description of the ephemeral trees which go back to the Alexander romances. 'And in that plain, every day at sun-rising, begin to grow small trees, and they grow till mid-day, bearing fruit, but no man dare take of that fruit, for it is a thing of faerie. And after mid-day they decrease and enter again into the earth, so that at the going down of the sun they appear no more. And so they do every day.' Next comes a description of Prester John's state when he went to war and when he rode privily. When he went to war he had carried before him three crosses of gold full of precious stones, each cross being carried in a chariot. The crosses were guarded by 10,000 men at arms and more than 100,000 foot soldiers, not counting the main host and wings, as ordained for battle. In peace-time the emperor had borne before him a plain cross of wood, in remembrance that Christ died upon a tree, together with a golden platter filled with earth, in token that Prester John's nobility and might, like his body, would turn to dust, but he had also borne before him a silver vessel full of precious stones to signify his lordship and might.

VII. 'MEN WHOSE HEADS DO GROW BENEATH
THEIR SHOULDERS'

From von Diemeringen's German translation, 1484.

(See p. 62).

IX. FLAT FACE
From Velser's German translation, 1482.
(See p. 63).

VIII. SCIAPOD
From von Diemeringen's German translation, 1484.
(See p. 55).

Prester John dwelt chiefly in his city of Susa. Here his palace was so noble and rich that no man could believe what was told of it unless he had seen it. Each tower of the palace was adorned with gold, and in each tower were two carbuncles, so disposed that they gave light at night. The gates were of sardonyx, and the borders and bars were of ivory. The windows were of crystal, and the tables were made of emeralds, amethysts and gold, covered with precious stones. The steps to the throne and the pillars of the hall were constructed of jewels, gold and orient pearls. There were no lamps in the palace, only carbuncles, to give light at night, while a brazier full of balm gave forth a sweet savour, and voided away all wicked airs and corruptions. Prester John's bed was made of sapphires, blended with gold, to induce sleep and to keep him from lechery: 'for he will not lie with his wives, but four sithes in the year, after the four seasons, and that is only for to engender children.' He was served by seven kings, seventy-two dukes and three hundred and sixty earls. Twelve archbishops and twenty bishops sat at his table, and the Patriarch of St. Thomas was his pope. Each of these great lords had his special duties. One was master of the household, another was his chamberlain, another held the dishes, another the cup; one was his steward, another his marshal and prince of arms. 'And his land dureth in very breadth four months' journeys, and in length out of measure, that is to say, all the isles under earth that we suppose to be under us.'

The emperor was called Prester John because of his great humility. Once upon a time there was a mighty prince, a paynim, who had Christian knights in his train. During his travels with one of his knights he reached Egypt where, in church on the Saturday in Whitsun-week, a bishop was busy with ordinations. The prince asked what kind of men they were who were before the bishop, and the knight answered that they were being ordained priests. Thereupon the prince said that he would no more be called emperor but priest, and

F

that he would take the name of the first priest who left the church. His name was John, and thereafter the rulers of that country were always called Prester John. The source of this legend has not been traced, but it fits into the picture as a whole. Avoiding many of the extravagances of the Letter, Mandeville has contrived to conjure up something of the wonder and mystery of the East. The story of this, the mightiest and saintliest of earthly rulers, with his pomp and humility, his hosts of retainers, his happy subjects and his busy cities, must have brought life and colour to many a dingy city of the west and given fresh courage and hope to hundreds in a world which was noisy with war and rumours of war. Somewhere, at the world's end, was this happy land, where Christians, Jews, Amazons and Brahmans could all live together in contentment and peace, where men had work and food and abundant leisure, and where none was downtrodden or oppressed. Here, at last, was the promise of that Earthly Paradise which hung over men's minds like a dream. Even if Mandeville failed to reach it, he could paint a picture which must have gripped the imagination of every reader. These chapters on the Great Chan and Prester John go far to explain the enduring popularity of Mandeville's book.

Mandeville now returns to Odoric for a description of the 'Old Man of the Mountain,' the chief of the Ismailites or Assassins. He had a stately castle with beautiful gardens and wells, and in his castle the chambers were all adorned with gold and azure. Here were also the fairest damsels under the age of fifteen years, and fair striplings, all clad in cloth of gold. Into this paradise of delights this wicked old man would entice young and lusty bachelors, and show them the conduits of milk and wine, and the damsels, while birds, moved by craft, sang gaily, and from a high tower came the sound of music so merrily that it was a joy to hear. He told his victims that that place was paradise indeed, and that the damsels were angels. Then he drugged the lusty bachelors and promised them that, if they would die for him, they would enjoy this paradise, and later find themselves in a fairer paradise, where they would see God in his majesty and bliss, and where they would live for ever, and that the maidens would play with them and still be maidens. Then, when they had recovered their senses, he sent them forth to slay some lord who was his enemy, hoping thus to be revenged on all his enemies. But his wicked plans miscarried. The Old Man's end was sudden and well deserved, for the worthy men of those parts besieged his castle, put him to death, and laid waste his paradise. 'And since that time,' adds Marco Polo (who devotes three chapters to the subject), 'he has had no successor; and there was an end of all his villainies.'

Most of my quotations have been from the Cotton version of the 'Travels,' but I close this chapter with the description of Prester John's kingdom and state from the Egerton text printed by Sir George Warner in 1889 for the Roxburghe Club. This version differs at times from the Cotton text. It omits some incidents and expands others; it is often more original in style, while the north-country words and phrases give it a charm of its own. Readers will note the personal touch at the end of the extract, which is not found in the Cotton version.

OF THE ROYAL ESTATE
OF
PRESTER JOHN

(From Chapter XXX of the Egerton Version)

(spelling modernized)

This Emperor Prester John has many diverse countries under his empire, in the which are many noble cities and fair towns and many isles great and large. For this land of Inde is departed in isles because of the great floods that come out of Paradise and run through his land and depart it. And also in the sea he has many great isles. The principal city of the isle of Pentoxore is called Nise; and there is the emperor's seat, and therefore it is a noble city and a rich. Prester John has under him many kings and many divers folk; and his land is good and rich, but not so rich as the land of the Great Caan of Cathay. For merchants come not so mickle to that land as to the land of Cathay, for it were too long way. And also merchants may find in the isle of Cathay all that they have need of, as spicery, cloths of gold and other rich things; and they let also for to go thither because of long way and great perils in the sea. For there are in many places in the sea great rocks of the stone that is called adamant, the which of his own kind draws to him iron; and for there should pass no ships that had nails of iron there away because of the foresaid stone, for he should draw them to him, therefore they dare not wend thither. The ships of that country are all made of wood and none iron. I was one time in that sea, and I saw as it had been an isle of trees and bushes growing; and the shipmen told me that all that was of great ships that the rock of the adamant had gert [caused to] dwell there, and of diverse things that were in the ships were those trees and those bushes sprung. And for these perils and such other, and also for the long way, they wend to Cathay. And yet Cathay is not so near that ne them behoves from Venice or from Genoa or other places of Lombardy be in travelling by sea and by land eleven months or twelve ere they may win to the land of Cathay. And yet is the land of Prester John mickle farther by many a day journey. And merchants that wend thither wend through the land of Persia and come to a city that men call Hermes, for a philosopher that men called Hermes founded it. And then they pass an arm of the sea and come to another city that is called Soboth or Colach; and there find they all manner of merchandise and popinjays as great plenty as is in our country of larks. In this country is little wheat or barley, and therefore they eat millet and rice, honey, milk and cheese and other manner of fruits. And from thence may merchants pass surely enough if them list. In that land are many popinjays, the which they call in their language psitakes; and they speak of their own kind as properly as a man. And those that speak well have long tongues and large, and upon either foot five toes: and they that speak not or else little have but three toes.

This ilk royal king Prester John and the Great Caan of Tartary are evermore allied together through marriage: for either of them weds other daughter or other sister. In the land of Prester John are great plenty of precious stones of diverse kinds, some of them so great and so large that they make of them vessels, as dishes, dublers, cups, and many other things that long were to tell.

Now will I speak of some of the principal isles of Prester John's land, and of the royalty of his state and what law and belief he and his people hold. This emperor Prester John is a Christian man, and the most part of his land also, if all it be so that they have not all the articles of our belief so clearly as we have. Not forby they trow in God, Father and Son and Holy Ghost; and full devout men they are and true ilk one to other, and there is nowhere with them fraud or guile. This emperor has under his subjection seventy-two provinces; and in ilk one of them is a king. And these kings have other kings under them, and all are tributaries to the emperor Prester John. In the land of Prester John are many marvels. But among other there is a great sea all of gravel and sand, and no drop of water therein. And it ebbs and flows as the great sea does in other countries with great waves and never more stands still without moving. That sea may no man pass, neither by ship nor otherwise; and therefore it is unknown to any man what kind land or country is on the other side of that sea. And if there be no water in that sea, nevertheless there is great plenty of good fish taken by the sea banks; and they are right savoury in the mouth, but they are of other shape than fishes are of other waters. I, John Mandeville, ate of them, and therefore trow it, for sickerly it is sooth.

And three day journeys from that sea are great hills, out of the which comes a great river that comes from Paradise; and it is full of precious stones, and no drop of water. And it runs with great waves through wilderness into the Gravelly Sea, and then are they no more seen. And this river runs ilk week three days so fast that no man dare come therein, but all the other days may men gang into it, when they will, and gather of the precious stones. And beyond that river toward the wilderness is a great plain among hills, all sandy and gravelly, in the which plain are trees as it seems, the which at the sun rising begin to grow and a fruit to spring out of them; and they grow so unto it be mid-day, and then begin they to dwindle and turn again to the earth, so that by the sun be set there is nothing seen of them, and thus they fare ilk a day. But of this fruit dare no man eat ne nigh it, for it seems as it were a phantom and a dessayuable [deceitful] thing to the sight. And this is holden a marvellous thing, and so it may well.

And in the foresaid wilderness are many wild men with horns upon their heads; and they dwell in woods as beasts and speak not, but grunt as swine do. Also in some woods of that land are wild hounds that never will come to man more than foxes will do in this country. And there are fowls also speaking of their own kind, and they will hail men that come through the deserts, speaking as openly as they were men. These fowls have large tongues and on either of their feet five nails. And there are others that have but three nails on either foot, and they speak not so well ne so openly. These fowls call they psitakes, as I said before.

This ilk great king and emperor Prester John, when he wends to battle against his enemies, he has no banner borne before him, but instead of banner there are borne before him three crosses of fine gold, the which are great and high and well dight with precious stones. And to the keeping of ilk a cross are ordained and assigned 10,000 men of arms and more than 100,000 men on foot, on the same manner as men keep a banner or a standard in battle in other places. And this number of men is alway assigned to the keeping of the foresaid crosses aye when the emperor wends to battle, without the principal host and without certain lords and their men that are ordained for to be in his own battle, and also without certain scales ordained for forraying. And when he rides in time of peace with his privy meinie, there is borne before him a cross of tree, without gold or painture or precious stones, in remembrance of Christ's passion that he suffered on a cross of tree. Also he has borne before him a plate of gold full of earth, in token that for all his great noblay and his lordship he came from earth and into earth shall he turn. And there is borne before him another vessel full of gold and of jewels and precious stones, as rubies, diamonds, sapphires, emeralds, topazes, crysolites, and other many, in token of his great noblay, lordship and might.

Now will I tell you the array of Prester John's palace, the which is commonly at the city of Suse. And that palace is so rich, so delightable and so noble, that it is wonder to tell. For above the principal tower are two pommels of gold; and in either of them are two carbuncles great and fair, the which shine right clear upon the night. And the principal gates of the palace are of precious stones, that men call sardonyx, and the bases of them are of ivory; and the windows of the hall and the chambers are of crystal. And all the tables on which they eat are of emeralds, amethysts and some of gold, set full of precious stones, and the pillars that bear the tables are of the same manner of precious stones. And the grees [steps] on which the emperor goes up to his throne where he sits at the meat, are one of onyx, another of crystal, another of jasper, another of amethyst, another of sardonyx, another of coral; and the highest gree, whereon he sets his feet at the meat is of chrysolite. And all these grees are bordered with fine gold, fret full of pearl and other

86

precious stones about the sides and the ends. And the sides of his throne are of emeralds bordered with fine gold, set full of precious stones. The pillars in his chamber are of fine gold set full of precious stones, of which many are carbuncles that give great light on nights; and yet nevertheless he has ilk a night burning in his chamber twelve vessels of crystal full of balm to give good smell and sweet and to drive away wicked air. And the form of his bed is all of sapphires, well bound with gold, for to make him to sleep well and for to destroy lechery; for he will not lie by his wives, but at four certain times in the year, and then all only for to get children.

This emperor has also another palace, rich and noble, in the city of Nise, and there he sojourns when him list; but the air is not so good there ne so wholesome as it is at Suse. Throughout all the land of Prester John they eat but once on the day, as they do in the court of the Great Caan. And ye shall understand that Prester John has ilk a day in his court eating more than 30,000 of folk, without comers and gangers; but neither 30,000 there nor in the court of the Great Caan spend so mickle meat on a day as 12,000 in our country. This emperor has also evermore seven kings in his court for to serve him; and when they have served him a month, they wend home and other seven kings come and serve another month. And with these kings serve alway seventy-two dukes and three hundred and sixty earls, and many other lords and knights. And ilk a day there eat in his court twelve archbishops and twenty bishops. And the Patriarch of Saint Thomas is there as it were pope. All archbishops and bishops and abbots there are kings and great lords of fees. And ilk one of them has some office in the emperor's court; for a king is porter, another hawler, another chamberlain, another steward of household, another butler, another server, another marshal, and so forth of all other offices that belong to his court; and therefore is he full richly served and worshipfully. His land lasts on breadth four month's journeys; and on length it is without measure. Trow all this for sickerly I saw it with mine eyes and mickle more than I have told you. For my fellows and I were dwelling with him in his court a long time and saw all this that I have told you and mickle more than I have leisure for to tell.

CHAPTER IX

The Valley Perilous

CHAPTER XXXI contains one of the most dramatic episodes in the book, the passage of the Valley Perilous or the Vale Enchanted. As recounted in the Cotton version, the valley lay between two mountains beside the isle of Mistorak (Malasgird, in Armenia) nigh to the river Phison, four miles in extent. It was full of tempests, thunderings and great noises as of tabors, nakers (drums) and trumps, as though a great feast were in progress, and it was the home of devils. Half way through the valley, under a rock, was the head and visage of a devil, full horrible and dreadful to see, beholding all comers with dreadful eyes, which moved and darted fire, and vomited smoke and fire and so much abomination that no man could endure it. Mandeville and his fellows were loath to enter this place, but there were with them two friars minor from Lombardy who said they would go in with the travellers, trusting upon God; and after Mass was said every man was shriven and houseled, and fourteen persons entered, of whom only nine emerged. Those lost were two of Greece and three Spaniards. The other members of the company went forward by another way. Once in the valley the travellers found hoards of gold, silver and jewels lying about which they dared not touch, as they feared that the devils had put them there to tempt covetous men. Dead bodies were lying by the way in such numbers that it seemed as if two mighty kings had fought a great battle there, and the bodies were whole, without rotting. Some were in the habits of Christian men, who appeared to have gone there to take the treasure, but

88

had perished through lack of faith. The travellers were thrown down and beaten many times by winds, thunder and tempests. But, God helping them, they passed through in safety.

This story is worked up almost literally from Odoric and the reference to the two friars may well have been inserted to anticipate a possible charge of plagiarism (see above p. 35). Yule thinks that Odoric's account may have been based on actual experience. That he passed through some real terror is obvious. Yule adds a long note suggesting that Odoric's valley, which lay by the River of Delights, may be the Regruwan, forty miles north of Kabul, in the Hindu Kush, crossed perhaps by Odoric on his way from Tibet, and that the River of Delights may be the Panchshir, which the Regruwan adjoins. There are gigantic rock figures in the same region, and modern travellers have described the sound of invisible drums heard in the deserts of Central Asia and elsewhere. It is interesting to note that Bunyan appears to have taken this story from Mandeville in his description of the Valley of the Shadow of Death.

The story as told in the Cotton and other versions was exciting enough. But, as time went on, apparently, the public was looking for something racier and more realistic, and they had not long to wait.

The Latin version, printed about 1484, without place or printer's name, called by Vogels and Warner the vulgate, tells the story twice over (in chapters XLIV and XLV). The first description starts soberly enough. It speaks of the thunder and the strange noises put forth by evil spirits, then describes the devil's head and the hoards of gold, silver and jewels displayed for the undoing of covetous men. It then adds a description (not mentioned in the English version) of certain evil spirits which terrified beholders in all kinds of horrid shapes, and chapter XLIV ends with the observation, also found in the English version, that Christian men could enter without peril, although sorely plagued and threatened.

Chapter XLV commences with the story of the two Franciscans, the two Greeks and the three Spaniards, who were lost, the hoards of gold and silver, the dead bodies, and then strikes fresh ground. The travellers were attacked by wild beasts like pigs, bears or goats, which ran between their legs and knocked them down. The air was full of lightening, thunder and hail. Mandeville and his fellows were struck and beaten on shoulders, back and loins, until they fell unconscious for one or two hours, but the visions disclosed to them between sleeping and waking could not be told, as the friars had said that they must never be revealed. Such was the force of the blows that Mandeville thought his head would fly from his body, and after eighteen years he still carried a mark which changed colour and threatened to remain with him to the end. The travellers pressed on, however, past the devil's head, once again threatened and thrown down by wild beasts, and even at the exit of the valley the devils still threatened and derided them. Finally, after walking for four leagues over dead bodies, this sorely-tried little company emerged from the valley and took shelter in some neighbouring dwellings, where they refreshed and bathed themselves.

Another Latin edition, printed at Antwerp [Gouda] c. 1485, gives much the same text, but contains frequent references, not found elsewhere, to Odoric. At the end of chapter XLIV this version actually incorporates the whole of Odoric's account, if not verbatim at least practically in the same words, with a pious reference to the friar's death and the face-saving remark: *non fuit tot perpessus in valle sicut Dominus Jo*.

For the most part the other versions follow the Latin text fairly closely. They all speak of the infernal orchestra, the hoards of demon treasure, the devil's head, the dead but unrotted bodies, the darkness, the wild beasts and the dolorous blows. But the French edition, printed at Lyons, in 1480, which follows fairly closely the earliest French text of 1371, adds the interesting information that, when plunged in darkness the travellers and the two friars declared that if they had been lords of the whole world they would gladly have renounced all their power and riches in order to be relieved of these dangers. The Latin version speaks of the travellers having been thrown down five hundred times; the French says more than a thousand times, and, when trampled on, the so-called dead bodies wailed and moaned most pitifully. The blows and beatings left each victim with a black mark the size of a hand. Mandeville's scar, which had been seen by many, remained with him until he repented of his sins and fell to his prayers, when it vanished miraculously, leaving the skin whiter than the rest.

The Dutch version (1470) and the Italian version of 1480 follow the French text closely. The German translation by Otto von Diemeringen (1484) gives a truly horrific picture of the devil's head (coloured in the British Museum copy and in the Fairfax Murray copy now in the Library of Congress), but adds little to the text. He gives details however of the injuries received. One had a weal as if he had been struck by a whip. Another had a mark on his forehead as if he had been branded. A third had a coal-black spot on his breast. And the others likewise, each having a mark a hand's breadth in size.

The German version by Martin Velser adds little of importance, but the description has a dramatic interest of its own. Velser thought, obviously, that the story needed corroboration. He must have heard of the suggestion that Odoric and Mandeville travelled together. Odoric was a friar. Velser therefore introduces a monk from an unknown monastery, who does not claim to have heard the story from Odoric himself — the dates would be against that — but who confirmed it as a tradition still preserved there among the brothers. I have translated the passage in full.

So one departs from the island called Millestrorothe which is on the left hand by the river Physon. There is a great marvel there, namely a valley between two mountains which extends for about three leagues, which is called the evil valley. Some call it the Dark Valley, and others the Valley of Thunder. In this valley are many dreadful and terrible things, great tempests of wind and lightening and mighty rocks, which are not to be described. At times one hears trumpets and at others drums. The Valley is indeed full of devils which are everywhere. And those of that country call it the anti-chamber of hell. In the valley there is great treasure of gold and precious stones, for which many persons have lost their lives for greed, for which they would otherwise not have risked their lives. In the middle of the Valley is a great rock, and on it is a devil's face, which is more horrible than anything one could find in the world. It is visible only as far as the breast. And I say that there is no man in the world so hardy, but that if he beholds it his heart would fail him for terror. It would seem to him as if he would perish and die of fright, for the figure seems as if it would eat one up forthwith, when it turns its eyes about, and shoots out stinking smoke and evil smells from its mouth. The mountains and rocks shake and quiver, and no living man can look at the face for sheer terror. But any good Christian, trusting in Christ and the holy Trinity, and having made his true confession, can traverse this valley. But without great fear and tribulation no one can come through it, for one sees evil spirits which terrify one in many ways, with hail and storms and thunder and lightening, fire and water. In addition there is darkness which makes a man lose his faith and think that God has forsaken him, and is about to take vengeance upon him.

But I Michel Velser, when I heard tell of this from this honourable knight, thought it incredible, until a barefoot monk came to me and said they had formerly in their monastery one who had also traversed this valley, and that what was related was in fact true. And they held him to be a pious and holy man, who swore by his office that he was to be believed. Then I believed, for this worthy knight has never been found to lie.

Now know that I John of Montevilla and my fellows were in great doubt when we approached the Valley, whether we should venture, trusting in God's mercy, to enter the Valley or not. One was for it, another against, and we could not agree. Then there came to us two monks of the Order of barefooted friars from Lombardy, who were true men. They said that if any one of us was hardy enough to pass through the Valley, they would teach us what to do and bear us company. The worthy brothers then gave us comfort, and we said that we would undertake the venture in God's mercy and with their support. They said mass, and we confessed and partook of the holy body of Jesus Christ, and prepared ourselves for the way. And know that when we entered the Valley we were thirteen, but when we came through the Valley we were nine only, and we knew not what happened to the other four. At first there were seventeen in our company, two from Greece and two from Spain. These we found at the end of the Valley, they having gone round it.

In the Valley we saw a great hoard of treasure, gold and silver and precious stones, but whether the treasure was put there to deceive us I do not know, for I touched none of it, for the devils are very cunning and deceitful, and often exhibit things that are not what they seem, wherefore people are often misled. Therefore I touched nothing lest I should leave my devotion, for I have never been afraid of death or had much concern for material things. We saw also a piteous collection of dead people who lay there, and, if two kings' armies had fought on that place, there could not have been more, which was a dreadful sight to see. I marvelled how the bodies could lie there without rotting, for some looked as if they had only recently been killed. I saw many lying there in the habits of Christian men. Indeed my heart was fearful and, for fear, I was constrained to pray. As one first enters the Valley there is a good road which continues for about half a league. Then it begins to grow dark, like the period of twilight, and when we had gone a league it was as dark as if we were in a cloud of fog. We saw neither stars nor sun. Then we came into utter darkness which lasted for a full league, and we knew not what was happening. Indeed we gave ourselves up for lost. We had never been in such tribulation in the world before, and if the whole world had been ours, we would gladly have surrendered it and become poor. It seemed as if we should never survive this marvel. In the darkness we were thrown down quite a hundred times and beaten, until our strength failed us. The Valley was full of black beasts, which ran between our legs and threw us down as often as we stood up. Then came a mighty rushing wind, with thunder and lightning, until it seemed to us that the world was about to end. And when we fell, we fell on dead men, and those that still lived began to wail, which was a great misery to hear. And it is my belief that, if we had not strengthened our hearts with the gentle and holy body of Lord Jesus Christ, we should all have been left in that Valley. But we did not escape without untold number of blows, so that we fell unconscious, and, but for the help of Almighty God, we should never have escaped. We saw many wonderful things which are not to be told, for it was not allowed. The monks from the monastery forbade us to tell it to anyone. Moreover, there was none among us but had a mark to show that he had been in that Valley. I had a mark on the neck, the result of a mighty and sudden blow, which I carred for eighteen years. It was a black mark, which was seen by many. But when I gave up my pride and began to be sorry for my sins and misdeeds, on the day when I returned to God, the black mark departed and my skin became white as before, although I was told that I should carry it to the end of my life. Therefore I counsel no man to traverse that Valley, since God might be displeased. And, as I have told you, when we were in the darkness we saw that hideous figure, and shortly after we saw the light of day. Then we all rejoiced and forgot our sufferings. As we came towards the light we were often thrown down by the wind and hail, also by evil fiends who attempted to do much to us. But God the Almighty delivered us at last with his mercy, and we came alive out of the Valley.

CHAPTER X

Giants, Brahmans, Gold-digging Ants, the Earthly Paradise, Tibet and other matters

HAVING escaped from the terrors of the Valley Perilous the traveller found himself at once in a land of giants. In a great isle beyond the Valley were giants thirty feet high, who ate gladly of men's flesh. But in another isle were giants more than eighty feet high. Both races were cannibals. Mandeville had no desire to go there and be devoured, but he claims to have seen giant sheep as great as oxen. As for the giants, he was content to take his information at second hand. 'And men have seen, many times, those giants take men in the sea out of their ships and brought them to land, two in one hand and two in another, eating them going, all raw and all quick.' Beyond that isle was another inhabited by cruel and evil women who slew men with a look, like basilisks. In another isle was a race of unpleasant people with strange and quite unmentionable wedding customs. The chief actors in these little domestic dramas were called 'fools of wanhope,' but readers who want to know what they did and why they were so called must turn to the text itself. I cannot possibly give it here. Not far off dwelt a simple folk who refrained from the flesh of hares, hens and geese and yet reared these creatures for the pleasure of looking at them. This passage, believe it or not, is taken, by way of Vincent of Beauvais,[1] almost verbatim from Caesar's account of the ancient Britons!

The description of the giraffe, which Mandeville calls

[1] *Spec. Hist.* I, ch. 91.

95

orafle or gerfaunt shows what a strange muddle Europeans made of the name. The creature is called variously cameleo-pardus, jiraffin, geranfalk and even seraph, and the description is often as wild as the name. Mandeville's account is as follows: 'that is a beast, pomely or spotted, that is but a little more high than is a steed, but he hath the neck a twenty cubits long; and his croup and his tail is as of an hart; and he may look over a great high house.' Other strange animals are mentioned, the chamelon, great serpents with crests on their heads and six feet, white lions, boars with six feet, and on every foot two large claws, and mice as great as hounds.

Chapter xxxii brings us to the island of Bragman, where lived the Brahmans. This chapter is worked up either from the apocryphal correspondence between Alexander the Great and the Brahman king Dindimus, by way of Vincent of Beauvais[1] or from Prester John's Letter, or both. When Alexander proposed to conquer the Brahmans they told him that he had riches enough. They drew attention to the simplicity of their lives, pointed out that they had no wealth for him to covet, asked him why he was so proud and fierce, and bade him contemplate his mortality. Whereat Alexander was abashed and confused, and departed from them. In the isle of Pytan dwelt the Astomi of Pliny and Vincent of Beauvais,[2] dwarfs who were nevertheless of good colour and shape, and who lived on the smell of wild apples. When they went travelling they had to take their apples with them, for if they lost the savour of the apples they died anon. In another island were people who lived on fish and were covered with fur from head to foot, the Ichthyophagi of the Alexander romances. The Egerton translator speaks of them as feathered, but that is his responsibility. In the desert, fifteen days journey from the river Beaumare (Buemar in the Epistle of Alexander), were the Trees of the Sun and the Moon, which spoke to

[1] *Spec. Hist.* IV, ch. 66–71.　　[2] *Spec. Hist.* I, ch. 93.

96

X. THE 'RYDINGE OF PRESTER JOHN.'

From a MS in the British Museum.

(See p. 80).

XI. THE DEVIL'S HEAD IN THE VALLEY
PERILOUS

From von Diemeringen's German translation, 1484.
(See p. 88).

Alexander and warned him of his death.[1] The men who kept the trees and ate the fruit lived for 400 or 500 years. Mandeville would have liked to see those trees, but the desert was full of dragons and serpents, elephants and unicorns and other savage beasts, so that an escort of 100,000 men-at-arms would be required and he had to rely on what 'was told us of them of the country.'

The story, as Alexander is made to tell it in his Letter to Aristotle, has a dignity and pathos of its own and is related at length by Warner.[2] Alexander was told, when in India, that ten days' journey from thence were two trees, speaking both Indian and Greek, the one, a male tree (of the Sun), the other a female tree (of the Moon). From these trees he would learn what good or evil should befall him. So, with guides and troops, Alexander journeyed through deserts infested with serpents and wild beasts till they came to the spot where they found the priest of the oracle, a man ten feet high, of sable hue, with teeth like a dog's, clothed in skins, and having pearls and rings hanging from his ears. He bade Alexander kiss the tree-trunks and pray for a truthful answer. Then, as the sun went down, the priest told them all to look upwards and to speak never a word. Alexander thought in his heart: 'Shall I return home to my mother and sisters in triumph when I have conquered the world?' A whisper came in the Indian language, 'Lord of the whole world thou wilt be, but to thine own land thou wilt not return alive.' Again, at the first rising of the moon, Alexander asked, but in thought alone, where he would die. The Tree answered in Greek that when May came round he would die in Babylon by a hand he suspected not. Whereupon Alexander and his companions wept and returned. The next morning they roused the priest at dawn and endeavoured to learn the name of the traitor against whom Alexander was to be on guard. But the Tree of the Sun refused to baulk the hand of fate and bade them depart,

[1] Vincent, *Spec. Hist.* IV, ch. 56. [2] Warner, p. 219.

revealing only that Alexander's death would be by poison, not by the sword, and telling him that his mother Olympias would perish shamefully and be exposed unburied to the birds and beasts.

Mandeville now approaches Taprobana, or Ceylon, 'that is full noble and full fructuous.' In that happy island there were two summers and two winters every year. But the chief attraction of Taprobana was that it contained the famous gold-digging ants of Herodotus. Mandeville probably took the story from Vincent of Beauvais,[1] Prester John's Letter or the Alexander romances, and a most entertaining story it is. Mandeville calls the ants pismires, and they were as large as great hounds. No one dared go near them. Mandeville does not endow them with six feet, wings and tusks greater then wild boars, as does Prester John's Letter, but they burrowed underground at night and rested during the day, and it was only by subtlety that the people of those parts could get the gold. They took mares with foals, loaded the mares with baskets and drove them out to pasture in the ant-fields, but the foals they kept at home. No self-respecting ant could abide to see an empty basket, and immediately set to work to fill it with gold. 'And when that the folk suppose that the vessels be full, they put forth anon the young foals, and make them to neigh after their dams. And then anon the mares return towards their foals with their charges of gold. And then men discharge them to get gold enough by this subtlety. For the pismires will suffer beasts to go and pasture amongst them, but no man in no wise.' This episode might have been expected to provide contemporary artists with a heaven-sent opportunity, but it is not depicted in von Diemeringen's German version, which has the finest illustrations I have come across. There is, however, a picture in the other German version by Martin Velser, whose artist was usually well up to his work, but it is something of a disappointment. The

[1] *Spec. Nat.* XX. ch. 134.

artist shows a number of diminutive ants crowding round a horse with panniers on its back, while the horse turns its head to see if the baskets are full. In the foreground is a foal, and at the side is one of the local inhabitants, standing much too near the scene of action for safety. One has only to turn to some of the pictures in Mr. Druce's article referred to in the note[1] to see what an imaginative artist could do with this story.

We are now approaching the Earthly Paradise, the only place untouched by Noah's flood. Mandeville did not reach it, not being worthy, but he knew the way there and was well informed as to its appearance. It was enclosed by a wall covered with moss, which stretched from south to north. There was only one entry, and this was closed by a wall of fire. Mandeville is once again relying on Vincent of Beauvais,[2] but much of what follows, except for the noise of the waters, seems to be original. All around were mountains, deserts, rocks and raging torrents. No one could cross the deserts and mountains, and as for the rivers, they raged so tempestuously that no ship could live there. The noise made men deaf. Many great lords had assayed to reach the spot, but they died of weariness, or were smitten with blindness or deafness, or drowned in the waves, 'so that no mortal man may approach to that place without special grace of God, so that of that place I can say you no more; and therefore I shall hold me still, and return to that that I have seen.'[3]

In chapter xxxvi, Mandeville transports us to Tibet, which he calls Rybothe. It was an island, subject to the Great Chan, and it was a good country, full of all manner of goods, wines, fruit and other riches. The country people lived in tents made of black fern, but the principal city, by which he must mean Lhasa, was walled and paved with

---

[1] *Antiquaries Journal*, III (1923), p. 347, 'The Ant Lion,' by G. C. Druce, F.S.A.

[2] *Spec. Hist.* I ch. 63.

[3] Here Mandeville is outdone by John de Hese, whose fictitious but amusing travels can be dated c. 1389. He claimed to have seen the walls of the Earthly Paradise shining like stars. Close by was the mountain which Alexander climbed when, having subdued the whole earth, he sought to levy tribute from paradise itself. Zarncke, II, p. 170.

black and white stones. The people were idolators, and the country was ruled by a potentate called Lobassy, who bestowed all the benefices and other dignities, and his subjects obeyed him as elsewhere they did the pope at Rome. Then follows a curious account of the funeral customs on the death of the father of a family. The priests cut off the dead man's head, but left the flesh to be devoured by birds of prey. The skull they cleaned and used as a drinking cup. Most of this comes from Odoric, with one or two variations, and a change in the name of the ruler, whom Odoric calls Lo Abassi, adding that the people have many other preposterous and abominable customs. The Tibetan method of disposing of their dead is confirmed from other sources, but it is quite useless to go to Mandeville or Odoric for any satisfactory account of Tibet. Indeed, it has been suggested that Odoric never reached Lhasa at all.

The book ends for all practical purposes with a description of a rich Chinaman, attended by fifty damsels, who served him by day and lay by him at night, singing to him when he was at meat, ministering to his pleasure, and waiting continually upon him. Because of his long nails he could do nothing for himself. He was as helpless as a child and as fat as a pig. His palace, with its grounds, was two miles in extent, and the pavement of the chambers was of gold and silver. In the gardens was a little mountain with a meadow by it, and in that meadow was a little toothill (or what our grandfathers would have called a gazebo) with towers and pinnacles of gold, where this helpless individual could disport himself and take his pleasure. Then follows a description of the cramped feet of the Chinese women. Odoric inserts all this between his account of Tibet and the 'Old Man of the Mountain,' and places the scene on the mainland of Manzi. Mandeville, following his usual practice, places it on an island. Then follows the epilogue — a moving passage — to which reference is made later (p. 161), and the book is finished.

CHAPTER XI

The Hereford Map

AT the end of the 'Travels' Mandeville is made to say that on his way home he showed his book to the pope at Rome (the pope was then at Avignon), who remitted it to his council to be examined, and that the council not only proved it to be true, but 'they shewed me a book, that my book was examined by, that comprehended full much more, by an hundred part, by the which the *Mappa Mundi* was made after.' This is from the Cotton version; Egerton adds that the book was in Latin 'and that book he showed me.' These statements occur, so far as is known, only in the English versions, and must have been interpolated by the English translator. It is hopeless to look for the book which contained stranger marvels than the 'Travels,' but is it possible to identify the *Mappa Mundi* ?

One's mind jumps naturally to the great map in Hereford Cathedral. This can be dated with some certainty in or near the year 1300.[1] It has already been noted that Mandeville's book must have been compiled after 1360. The dates therefore present no difficulty. The map is the work of Richard de Haldingham and de Lafford, who held the prebend of Lafford in Lincoln Cathedral up to 1283, after which he held the stall of Norton at Hereford Cathedral. He was afterwards Archdeacon of Reading. The insignificance of Hereford, as pictured on the map, compared with Lincoln,

---

[1] Bevan & Phillott, *Medieval Geography* (1873), p. 6. Bevan & Phillott's book was accompanied by a large coloured reproduction of the map, which has been used for this present study. The map has recently been cleaned and remounted, and it is hoped that a new coloured reproduction may be issued by the Royal Geographical Society. See G. R. Crone, *The Hereford World Map*, 1948.

suggests that the map was drawn at Lincoln. However, this point is not material to our present enquiry. Drawn on a sheet of vellum the map is 54 inches in breadth by 63 inches in its extreme height. It is brightly coloured, although some of the colours have faded. Unlike other medieval maps, it is not an exercise in cartography but a picture book. It was intended to present to ordinary people in a direct and simple manner the marvels and wonders of the great world they could not hope to see for themselves, but with which they were familiar from stories taken from classical and later writers, from the Alexander romances and similar works, and to drive home in pictorial form the teachings of the Church.

It is difficult to believe that an Englishman writing in the fourteenth century of a *Mappa Mundi* can have been thinking of any other map. Bevan and Phillott give details of other medieval picture maps, but in point of size and elaboration of the pictorial illustrations, and in its ornamentation, the Hereford map is unsurpassed by anything that preceded it. Much of the material used by Mandeville is incorporated in it. This, of course, is not conclusive, as the same wonders and marvels were part of the common stock at that time, and are represented in other medieval maps, but there was nothing in England to equal the giant 'wheel' at Hereford.[1]

In this map the earth is represented as round in form and surrounded by the ocean. The east is at the top. Rather more than half the Map is devoted to Asia. Europe is on the left hand and Africa on the right. Jerusalem, as might be expected, is in the centre. The Earthly Paradise (which, it may be remembered, Mandeville did not reach, not being worthy, although he knew the way there), is shown at the top of the map surrounded by a lofty wall, from which flames burst forth. Mandeville writes that the wall stretched

---

[1] See Bevan & Phillot, p. xxii, & Beazley, *Dawn of Modern Geography*, II, p. 549, III, p. 528.

from south to north, 'and it hath not but one entry that is closed with fire, burning.' Adjoining is the Arbor Sicca, or Dry Tree, which Mandeville places in the Vale of Hebron. This tree went back to the beginning of the world and bore leaves until the Crucifixion, when it died, as did all the trees in the world. But when the Holy Land was again in the possession of Christian men it would wax green and bear fruit. Some account of this tree is given at p. 47.

A little below the Dry Tree is the word India written across the map. Beneath the first letter is a fine specimen of a sciapod, a creature with one leg and an enormous foot which it used as a kind of natural umbrella to shield it from the sun. It was a favourite monster with medieval artists. Mandeville places it in Ethiopia, a country frequently confounded with India as the home of marvels, and describes it as follows: 'In that country be folk that have but one foot, and they go so blyve that it is a marvel. And the foot is so large, that it shadoweth all the body against the sun, when they will lie and rest them.' Beneath the N of India are four pigmies clad in long cloaks and wearing round hats. Mandeville describes them as only three spans high, but right fair and gentle. They married and had children at the age of six months, but did little work, having giants in their service who tilled the land and laboured among the vines.

Just below the sciapod are two strange creatures called Gangines. These were dwarfs, but not as small as pigmies. They lived on the smell of apples, according to Mandeville. In the Map two Gangines are shown beneath an apple tree, and one is inhaling his daily food. Not far off, below the second I in India, is a parrot or popinjay which Mandeville found in the court of the Great Chan, a 'well speaking' bird, and not far off is a fine specimen of an elephant complete with castle on its back, of which, according to Mandeville, the King of Java had 14,000 ready for war. In the centre there is one of Mandeville's cockodrills (not shown weeping), and further to the left is a pelican feeding its young with its blood, with a fine golden ring round its neck. On the rim of the 'wheel' are two more human monsters, one a creature with horses' feet ('strong, mighty and swift runners'), the other a creature 'with great ears and long, that hang down to their knees.' In the Map the ears reach down to the ground and practically envelop the whole body, but something must be allowed for artistic licence. A little below is a wall with four turrets, behind which were the Ten Tribes and the cannibal nations, shut up behind the Caspian Mountains by Alexander the Great.

On the other side of the Caspian Sea is Mandeville's Gate of Hell, with flames bursting forth, a reference perhaps to the not yet extinct volcano Demavend, and just below is a striking picture of a gryphon or griffin, half eagle, half lion, stronger than eight lions and a hundred eagles, 'for one griffin there will bear, flying to his nest, a great horse, if he may find him at the point, or two oxen yoked together as they go at the plough.' This was the famous roc or rukh, familiar to us all from Sinbad's adventures in the 'Arabian Nights.' Not far off is a picture of a cannibal feast (Mandeville has much to say about cannibals), and nearer the centre of the map is Noah's Ark, neatly placed on the top of Mount Ararat, with Mr. and Mrs. Noah and some of the animals looking out of a window. Unfortunately the hole mentioned by Mandeville, through which the fiend escaped when Noah said *Benedicite*, is not shown. The medieval fortress close by is the Tower of Babel, and a little higher up is the Patriarch Abraham looking out of a window at Ur of the Chaldees. Mandeville knew the way to the Tower of Babel, but no man could reach it because of the dragons and serpents in the deserts thereabouts. Passing now into Syria, by way of Damascus, to the Dead Sea, Sodom and Gomorrah are indicated by walls and towers, and not far off is Lot's wife, a forlorn figure 'in likeness of a salt stone,' gazing back at the two cities. In Egypt the Nile makes a great show, and in one arm of the river, represented as a long, low barn, are the Granaries of Joseph, as the Pyramids were then called. Mandeville calls them Joseph's Garners, and denies that they were the tombs of great men, for tombs would not be void within, 'ne they should have no gates for to enter within.'

Ethiopia was a land of strange marvels, and has as fine a collection of monsters as could be found anywhere. Here also are the gold-digging ants to which Mandeville devotes a most amusing passage.[1] He calls them pismires, and places them in Ceylon. The fact that he got the story from Herodotus, by way of Vincent de Beauvais, is of no importance, for whatever Mandeville touched he made his own.

The Ethiopian monsters include people with one leg, one-eyed giants, four-eyed giants, creatures without heads, with eyes and mouths in their chests, creeping folk, men with a round hole in place of a mouth, who sucked their food through a pipe, men without ears, hermaphrodites, cave-dwellers who hissed like snakes, and creatures with one huge lip 'that when they sleep in the sun they cover all the face with that lip." Mandeville mentions all these human monstrosities and some others, adding a number of picturesque and, at times, intimate details which cannot be mentioned here, although the artist had no such scruples. But the dog-headed creatures, which Mandeville found in one of the Nicobar islands, are transported by the map-maker to the shores of the Baltic, where other medieval writers profess to have found them. Next come the strange people, who tested the legitimacy of their offspring by offering them to serpents 'for, if they be born in right marriage, the serpents go about them, and do them no harm, and if they be born in avoutry, the serpents bite them and envenom them. And thus many wedded men prove if the children be their own.' The map shows this process in active operation, with the mother anxiously watching her offspring in the embrace of writhing serpents.

[1] See above p. 98.

These then are the chief resemblances between Mandeville's 'Travels' and the Hereford *Mappa Mundi*. Their effect is cumulative and highly significant, but not conclusive. Still, the fact remains that an Englishman, having completed a translation of Mandeville, and being confronted with the Hereford Map, may well have been amazed to find that the one was in effect supplemental to the other. Detach some thirty-five or forty pictures from the Map, reproduce them separately, and they become a set of illustrations for Mandeville, so apt for their purpose that all that is necessary is to fit them into their places in the text.

CHAPTER XII

Outremeuse
and the Ogier Interpolations

JEAN D'OUTREMEUSE, the Liége notary, to whom reference has already been made, haunts the Mandeville student like a spectre. One can never be sure where he is, or when he will appear, but he is behind the scenes all the time, and seems to take a puckish delight in manifesting himself at awkward moments, and in disappearing behind his defences when we are most in need of him. Outremeuse is responsible for the statement that de Bourgogne on his death-bed declared himself to be Mandeville. We know that Outremeuse was Mandeville's executor, and that he acquired some of Mandeville's jewels. We may assume that he possessed himself of his testator's library, an important acquisition if, as I suspect, he re-issued his own versions of the 'Travels.' That Outremeuse had something to do with some versions of Mandeville is clear, but so far Hamelius, whose edition of the Cotton version was published in 1919, is the only scholar who regards Outremeuse as the author of the whole book. Hamelius states boldly on his titlepage, 'Mandeville's Travels, translated from the French of Jean d'Outremeuse.' In my view this goes much too far. If Mandeville's book was written in or about 1360, Outremeuse would then have been in his early twenties! As to Outremeuse's association with the book, some versions, to the surprise of most students of Mandeville, contain a number of highly-coloured stories of Ogier the Dane, which have no place in a book purporting to have been written by an Englishman, and which are quite clearly interpolations. Ogier the Dane has been identified with the Frankish hero Autcher, whose deeds were sung in French and German, but it is doubtful whether he had any connection with Denmark. He probably hails from the Ardennes. Ogier revolted against Charlemagne, fled to Lombardy and resisted the imperial forces for seven years. He was at last taken prisoner and imprisoned at Rheims. He was released in order to fight against the Saracen giant Brehus, or Braihier, after which he had a conqueror's career in the East. He was then carried off by Morgan la Fay, who made him immortal, and he either still lives at Avalon, or sleeps in a mountain, like Barbarossa, ready to be awakened in time of need. Most of his exploits are recorded by Outremeuse in his *Myreur*, and, if my theory is correct, he transferred them, or some of them, to Mandeville's 'Travels.' It must not be forgotten that Outremeuse wrote a poem, now lost, on Ogier. So much for the hero, now for the chronicler.

Outremeuse was a clerk and notary at Liége. He was born in 1338 and died in 1399. He wrote a long poem on the history of Liége, and an enormous prose work, the *Myreur* which was printed in six volumes in 1864-67. There is another work by Outremeuse, 'Le Trésorier de Philosophie Naturelle,' in manuscript at Paris,[1] which contains an interesting reference to Mandeville. The author cites among philosophers a 'noble homme, seigneur Jehan de Mandeville, chevalier, seigneur de Monfort, de Castelperouse, et de l'isle de Campdi, qui fut en Orient et es parties par della par longtemps, si en fist ung lappidaire selon l'oppinion des Indois.' It is not necessary to say more about this lapidary, except that a French version was printed under Mandeville's name at Lyons in 1530.

Outremeuse quotes several passages from this work in Latin, and tells us that Mandeville had lived in Alexandria (as *bailli*) for seven years, and that a Saracen there had given

---

[1] Bibl. Nat. fonds franc. 12,326: 16th century.

him some fine jewels, which passed subsequently into
Outremeuse's possession.

There is no reference to Mandeville in the *Myreur*, as
printed by Borgnet and Bormans, a strange omission when
one considers how much the *Myreur* owes to the 'Travels,'
but a MS which came to light in 1903 now supplies a con-
necting link. This MS was known to Borgnet, but its then
owner refused to allow it to be used. It was sold in 1903 and
acquired by the Bibliothèque Royale, Brussels (MS II,
3030). It is a fifteenth century MS. Book II is more complete
than in the MS used by Borgnet and is of particular importance for the years A.D. 794 to 826. A summary is given by
Louis Michel in 'Les Légendes épiques Carolingiennes dans
l'oeuvre de Jean Outremeuse,' Liége, 1935. On folio 405^R
appears a passage of which the following is a translation.

> This country of India and Ethiopia is a varied place according to
> the chronicles and according to what is recounted by Maître Jehan
> de Mandeville, knight, lord of Campoli, of Montfort and of Case
> Perouse, in his writings which he made of this country of India and
> of the parts where he was living a long time, more than thirty-three
> years, returning from thence the year of the nativity of our Lord
> Jesus Christ 1316 (sic), in which writings he recounts all that Ogier
> conquered and did during his time.[1]

So far as Ogier's exploits are concerned, Mandeville of
course did nothing of the kind. It was Outremeuse who
recounted all these things, and it was Outremeuse who
subsequently fathered them on Mandeville, salving his
conscience with the half-hearted acknowledgment already
referred to.

But to start at the beginning. Outremeuse's first move,
apparently, was to incorporate whole passages from Mandeville's 'Travels' into his *Myreur*, substituting Ogier for

---

[1] 'Cil pays d'inde et d'Ethioppie est ung diverse lieu, selonc les croniques et selonc
ce que mestre Jehan de Mandeville, chevalier, sire de Canpoli, de Montfort et del
Case Perouse, raconpte en ses escrips qu'il fist de ce pays d' Inde et des partiez où
il fut régnant loing temps, plus de xxxiii ans, et revint par dessa l'an de nativiteit
nostre Seigneur Jhesu Crist xiii c et xvi, où il raconpte tout ce que Ogier conquist
et fist à son temps.'

Mandeville. A large part of Book III of the *Myreur* (pp. 57–68 in Borgnet's edition) is nothing more or less than a 'potted' version of the 'Travels' from chapter XVIII onwards. After various hair-raising adventures, Ogier reaches the land of Lomb and the Pepper Forest, which, like Mandeville, he found to be eighteen journeys in length. Here Ogier builds the two cities Flandrine and Zinglantz, which he calls Flandrine and Florentine after his grand parents. Ogier mentions the serpents to be found in the forest, but omits Mandeville's story that the inhabitants burnt the pepper in order to destroy the serpents. Ogier and his companions also drank of the Fountain of Youth on the mountain of Polombe. Mandeville, it will be remembered, felt better after the draught. So did Ogier. It was only later that he attained immortality. At Calamye, in the kingdom of Mabaron, where was the body of St. Thomas the Apostle, the description of the church and the tomb come almost word for word from Mandeville. The island of Lamary, a hot country where men and women went naked and all the women were used in common, Cathay, the Land of Prester John, the Gravelly Sea, the two-headed geese, the vegetable lamb, the trees bearing meal, honey and venom, the bearded ladies in the land of Lomb, the Earthly Paradise, the Valley Perilous, Gog and Magog, the griffins, the Brahmans, the ephemeral trees and the Trees of the Sun and the Moon, all appear in their proper order, with added details in glorification of Ogier, whose business in life was conquest and the conversion of the heathen. If the captured rulers declined the benefits of Christianity they were quickly disposed of. The King Ganges for instance, an obstinate and disbelieving potentate, was promptly drowned in the river of that name. Nor are human monsters neglected. This part of the *Myreur* is in fact a masterpiece of adaptation and compression.

Outremeuse's next move, as it seems to me, was to take Mandeville's text and interpolate the Ogier stories. In the standard versions of Mandeville — French, English, Dutch, Spanish and Italian — there is not a single reference to Ogier, and it may be doubted whether Mandeville had ever heard of him. Heroes were not much in Mandeville's line. He mentions two only, Charlemagne and Alexander the Great, and then only in passing. To bring in Ogier in passage after passage, to explain his marvels and justify the christianizing of the East, would have been out of keeping with the whole character of the book. But for Outremeuse, with copies of Mandeville's 'Travels' at his disposal, a priceless opportunity presented itself. Most of Outremeuse's lost poem on Ogier seems to have found its way into the *Myreur*,[1] Nothing could have been easier than for Outremeuse, with his head full of Ogier, to insert the Ogier stories in the versions of Mandeville which he had at hand, and put them into circulation. If this is so, we have three versions of the text for which Outremeuse was largely responsible, the version used by von Diemeringen for his German translation, the abridged Latin vulgate text of c. 1484, and a manuscript at Brussels (Bibl. Royale 10420). So far as the vulgate edition is concerned, Outremeuse, in my view, was responsible for the whole of it. The printed edition has a most significant *Incipit*. It states that the book was first written in French by the knight, its author, in 1355 in the city of Liége, and shortly afterwards in the same city, translated into Latin.[2] This is the earliest text so far discovered which contains Ogier interpolations. They are not so detailed as in von Diemeringen's translation or in Brussels 10420, and it looks to me as if Outremeuse had tried his hand at an abridged Latin Ogier version in order

---

[1] It is interesting to note that Borgnet (Introd. p. xviii) found in the *Myreur* 105 instances of rhyme, of which 29 can be found in the "Gestes de Liége," while the remaining 76 occur in the Ogier passages. It looks as if Outremeuse was in such a hurry when working on his *Myreur* that he had no time to turn his verse into prose.

[2] Ferd. Henaux (*Bull. de l'inst. Archéol, Liégois*, IV (1850), p. 159, says that Mandeville caused a Latin translation of his work to be made by a Liége clerk, but no authority is given for the statement. Warner, p. xxxviii.

to test the market. Here, as in other interpolated texts, Ogier is introduced without rhyme or reason, not only in the Far East, which was the scene of his principal triumphs, but even in the Holy Land, where he converts the Saracens from their false doctrines. But in the East he really comes into his own. In Ind the More, in the land of Lomb, at Mabaron, in Mancy in China, in the Great Chan's own country of Cathay, in the Land of Prester John, in Ceylon, the story is always the same. Ogier marches in with his conquering heroes, subdues all non-christian peoples from sun-rising to sun-setting, builds cities, founds churches and abbeys, and divides up his conquests among his followers. It is even claimed that Prester John himself was descended from one of Ogier's lords. Only once, apparently, did he face disaster. His army was suffering from famine, but an angel showed him the famous trees bearing meal, honey and wine, and produced a miraculous draught of fishes, and all was well. Nor were his exploits likely to be forgotten. The standard versions of Mandeville tell us that in the palace of the King of Java there were pictures of the noble deeds done by knights in battle, wrought in gold and silver and precious stones. Here was an opportunity not to be missed. In the Latin vulgate edition the pictures showed the noble deeds of Ogier who, with force of arms, conquered all parts beyond the seas, from Jerusalem to the Trees of the Sun and the Moon, and even to the gates of the Earthly Paradise itself.

I have already referred to the significant *Incipit* in the vulgate Latin version, and have suggested that Outremeuse was the translator. There are many indications which support this view, but one example will suffice, the origin of the name of Prester John, a story with a curious development, which can be traced step by step through the Latin vulgate text to its final form in von Diemeringen's translation. The story as given in the Cotton and other standard texts is as follows (I quote from Pollard's edition, p. 197).

It was sometime an emperor there, that was a worthy and a full noble prince, that had Christian knights in his company, as he hath that is now. So it befell that he had great list for to see the service in the church among Christian men . . . And so it befell that this emperor came with a Christian knight with him into a church in Egypt. And it was the Saturday in Whitsun-week. And the bishop made orders. And he beheld and listened the service full tentively. And he asked the Christian knight what men of degree they should be that the prelate had before him. And the knight answered and said that they should be priests. And then the emperor said that he would no longer be clept king ne emperor, but priest, and that he would have the name of the first priest that went out of the church, and his name was John. And so evermore sithens, he is clept Prester John.

In the vulgate text the story is told quite differently (ch. XLI). Outremeuse omits the story as told in the standard version and introduces a new one based on his own *Myreur*. After relating how Ogier with his barons and armies had conquered the countries of the Great Chan and all India, he continues:

'There was among the barons one named John, the son of Goudebuef, King of Frisia, and the said John was devoted to God. When opportunity occurred he was wont to enter the thresholds of churches, for which reason the barons, as in jest, gave him the name Prester John. After Ogier had conquered the aforesaid regions he divided them among fifteen of his followers, and established whom he pleased from among them in his place and made him king, so that the Christian religion might be established there for ever. He delivered upper India to Prebyster John . . . for which cause all his successors in India are called Presbyter John.'

In the *Myreur* (III, p. 52) the story is told more briefly but the gist of it is there:

'And the king Goudebuef of Frisia delivered to him (Ogier) Prebyster John his son. He was called priest, because he went every day to pray in church and knelt in devotion before every altar. He was accustomed to call himself Prester John and was king of India because Ogier crowned him.'

The next development is found in Brussels 10420, by

which time, if I am right, Outremeuse was finding his feet
and had decided that his *Myreur* needed pushing. At folio
135[vo], after the passage giving the reason for Prester John's
name, as contained in the Cotton version, Brussels 10420
continues as follows :

'And while I lived there I found the contrary . . . *in a very
beautiful chronicle which is in India, in the city of Nyse*, which
reports that in the year 816 the aforesaid Ogier the Dane
of Denmark, and with him 20,000 men, conquered all the
country of Prester John and that which the Grand Chan
holds, and gave it to his princes . . . And among the other
princes he had one who was son to king Goudebuef of
Frisia, who went willingly to church, so that it occurred
to the princes to make a priest of him. And therefore he was
called Prester John. And Ogier gave him the land of India,
and so it was, and he was the first king that believed in God.
And therefore all the kings after him have the name of
Prester John, whatever may be their own name.'[1]

All this appears in the *Myreur* (the nickname, III, p. 52;
the coronation, p. 66), but the Brussels version is much
expanded, and for the first time we have a reference to the
mysterious chronicle preserved in Prester John's city. Can
this be anything but a direct reference to the *Myreur*?

The story as given in the German translation by Otto
von Diemeringen, Canon of Metz (who must obviously
have been at work on a manuscript in which Outremeuse
had thrown off all restraint, for it contains no less than
twenty separate Ogier references). After an account of
Ogier's triumphs in the East, von Diemeringen proceeds
(Book III, ch. IV):

'Here it should be noted how the name Prester John came
first into being. Ogier had a friend who was called King
Godebuch of Frisia. He had a son called John. This same
John was always to be found in churches: he prayed much

---

[1] See extract I printed at the end of this chapter. The reference to the "Ystor," in
extracts 3 and 4 should be noted.

and was very devout and performed many excellent priestly duties. And therefore, because he was so pious and was so often in church, he became a jest to other people. And therefore he was called Prester John. Now it happened that this same John performed many doughty deeds, so that he grew in favour with his cousin Ogier who, when he departed, bestowed upon him the lands he had won, and Prester John retained these same lands, and the name remained, so that all his descendants are so called to this day. Thus was a jest turned to earnest. *All this I read in that same country, in the Chronicles, which are preserved in the town of Nyse, in Our Lady's Minster*, and I believe none other than that the name itself came in this manner. But some say . . . [Then follows the story as given in the Cotton version, the translator adding that Prester John caused himself to be ordained priest]. But I prefer to believe the first story, which I have read in the books.'

Thus the whole story is complete. First, the tentative version in the Latin vulgate text, then the expanded story in Brussels 10420 with a reference to the Book of Chronicles, and, finally, still further expanded in the translation by von Diemeringen (who gives both stories), with the added information that the famous Book of Chronicles was preserved in Our Lady's Minster in Prester John's capital. All these stories point back to the *Myreur*, and that Outremeuse was responsible for them cannot now, I think, be questioned.

Brussels 10420 is written in an untidy and often illegible hand, and seems to belong to the late fifteenth or early sixteenth century. Judging by the carelessness of the writing, it would seem to have been produced, not commercially, but for private use. It is written in a French-Flemish dialect, the dialect in fact in which Outremeuse wrote the *Myreur*. There are no illustrations. The MS contains four Ogier passages, and is the only French text at present known to contain any Ogier references at all. I give the passages in full at the end of this chapter, partly to save students the labour of deciphering this incredibly corrupt manuscript, and partly because the French-Flemish dialect in which it is written has an important bearing on the problem.

Unfortunately, we shall probably never solve the question of the true relationship between Jean d'Outremeuse and Mandeville, but I am convinced that the real clue lies in the *Myreur*. The Ogier stories cannot be accounted for in any other way. Why an author, claiming to be an Englishman, should bother his head over a hero of whom he probably knew little, purporting to come from a country of which he knew less, has never been explained. The exploits have nothing to do with the narrative and are obviously interpolated. Everything points to Outremeuse as their author.

The extracts which follow contain two further references to the mysterious Chronicle, not found in the Latin vulgate text, and a story (extract 4) about Ogier's immortality which, as we shall see later, is still further developed by von Diemeringen. It is interesting to note that the Latin vulgate text, which I regard as Outremeuse's first venture, is much more restrained when dealing with the story that Ogier was still alive. It says merely (ch. XLVII) that some through folly or levity think that Ogier still lives on earth, but that it is wiser to believe that one who laboured so hard for Christianity must now reign with Christ in heaven. This was a bad lapse. It was at variance with the story in the *Myreur*, and it had to be corrected.

EXTRACTS FROM BRUSSELS 10420

1. Pollard, p. 197. After the passage giving the reason for Prester John's name, Brussels 10420, fo. 135v° adds, *Et quant je vivais la je trovay le contraire en seauz de pays et en un moult beal cronicle qui est en Ynde en la cite de Nyse, qui dist que l'an VIII° and XVI passat la meir le deseurdi Ogier ly Danois de Danemarche, et aveuc luy XX^m hommes, et conquist tout ce*

pays que Priest Johan tient et que li grand Can tient, si le donnat a ses princes. . . . Et entre les autres princes ilh avoit un qui astoit fils de roy Gondebuef de Frise et aloit volentiere a mostier (Moustier in *Myreur*, III, p. 52 — Minster). *Si le misent les prinches quilh feroient de lui ung prest. Et puis ilh fut nommeis Prest Johan. Et lui donat Ogier la terre dynde, sy en fut, et fut li premiere roys qui creist en dieu. Et partant tous li rois apres ont a nom Prestre Johan, quelle nom quilh ayent.*[1]

2. Pollard, p. 179. 'The Emperor Prester John taketh always to his wife the daughter of the Great Chan, and the Great Chan also, in the same wise, the daughter of Prester John. For these two be the greatest lords under the firmament.'

Brussels 10420, fo. 114v° adds: *car il le commandat Ogier li Danois quant ilh conquit les xviii royaulmes Ynde et Cathay et ilh li fist par fait que sy il* (sic) *ne guerroient mais amis fuissent lun a lautre.* [For so it was ordained by Ogier the Dane when he conquered the XVIII kingdoms of India and Cathay, and he did it in order that they should not engage in war, but be friends, the one to the other:] In the *Myreur* (III, 66) Ogier makes Prester John king of India. The story of the marriage is not in the *Myreur* as we have it.

3. Pollard, p. 179. 'This Emperor Prester John is a Christian, and a great part of his country also.'

Brussels 10420, fo. 114v° adds, *Et le fut jadis tous quant Ogier ly Dannois deseurdis les conquist et les convertit, ainsy quilh soutiennent en lour ystor* — a clear reference to Outremeuse's own *Myreur*. [And all were such (i.e., Christians) aforetime, when Ogier the Dane beforementioned conquered and converted them, as they maintain in their history.]

4. Pollard, p. 196. After describing the Trees of the Sun and the Moon, which warned Alexander of his death, and stating that men who ate of the fruit and of the balm of those trees lived for four or five hundred years, Brussels 10420, fo. 134v° adds, *Et sachies que Ogier li Danois y fut et*

---

[1] For translation, see p. 114.

gostat du bosme. Et partant ilh dient en ce pays qu'ilh vistat [vécut]
tant. Et est en lour ystorie comme dieu li otriat [octroyait] quilh
visfreroit jusques a tant quilh demandroit la mort quant ilh
respentat Charlot de Franche sa mort. Mais ilh dient que c'est
par le bosme qu'ilh gostat la. [Know that Ogier the Dane was
there, and tasted of the balm. And therefore they say in
that country that he still lives. And it is (recorded) in their
history how God ordained that he should live until such
time as he called for death, when he should repent of the
death of Charlot of France. But they say that this is due
to the balm that he tasted there.]

It looks as if Outremeuse had written from memory and
forgotten the Charlot episode as related in the *Myreur*
(III, p. 162). It is related there that Charlot, bastard son of
Charlemagne, killed Ogier's bastard son, Bauduinet. After
various vicissitudes, Charlot was delivered by his father
Charlemagne to the bereaved Ogier (III, p. 277), who at first
intended to kill him, but afterwards pardoned him at the
command of St. Michael (III, p. 294). Charlot is ultimately
killed, not by Ogier, but by Huon of Bordeaux (III, p. 485).

Brussels 10420 has another contribution to make to the
Mandeville problem. At the end there is a reference to the
elusive 'John with the Beard.' It will be remembered that
in Book 4 (now lost) of the *Myreur* there is a statement that
it was Jean à la Barbe who confided to Outremeuse on his
deathbed in 1372 that his real name was Mandeville. The
other story was that Mandeville wrote his book at the instigation of a physician known as Jean à la Barbe. The
passage in the Brussels MS is as follows:

. . . *Dedens le noble cite de Liége en j hosteit en la basse*
sauenier que ons dit al hoste herbin levo ou je gisoy malaide, sy
men visentoit j venerable homme [et discret maistre Jehan a la
Barbe] phisechiens ly quis moy metit en la voye de fair chi liure et
moy cognut. 'In the noble city of Liége I lived in a house, in
the district of Basse Savenier, of Herbin Levo, where I lay
sick. Here I was visited by a worshipful man [and discreet,

Master John à la Barbe], a physician, who put me in the way of writing this book, and knew me.' Now Hamelius prints this passage in his edition of Mandeville (note to p. 210, line 33), but omits the words in brackets. This may have been due to oversight, but, had Hamelius quoted the extract in full, it would have done much to demolish his theory that the 'Travels' were written by Outremeuse, and not by Mandeville, alias de Bourgogne, alias 'à la Barbe.'

On this subject I will say one final word. No one who has studied Outremeuse's *Myreur* with any care can fail to be impressed by the author's verbosity and lack of method. Now there is nothing verbose or untidy about Mandeville. His book is a compact and straightforward narrative of travel, to my mind quite beyond the capacity of a writer such as Outremeuse.

The main points which I wish to make about Brussels 10420 are as follows:

1. For the first time we have a French text with Ogier passages.

2. The MS is in the same Flemish-French dialect as the *Myreur*, two noticeable characteristics of which are the spelling of 'il' as 'ilh' and the soft 'c' as 'ch.'

3. It is a late copy of a MS of the 'Travels' which passed through Outremeuse's hands. It marks stage 2 in the development of the Ogier interpolations, all, or most of which, can be traced back to the *Myreur*, and are clearly the work of Outremeuse.

BOOK THREE

The Book and what became of it

*

CHAPTER XIII

Manuscripts and Printed Editions

(GENERAL SURVEY)

THE existing manuscripts are said to number some 300. There are versions in Spanish, Dutch, Walloon, German, Bohemian, Danish and Irish. As evidence of the popular demand for wonders and marvels it is interesting to observe that only seventy-seven manuscripts of Marco Polo are known to exist, and that according to Warner the proportion in the British Museum was, in his time, twenty-nine of Mandeville to seven of Marco Polo. Others have been added in recent years, and the British Museum has now ten French Mandevilles, ten English, seven Latin, three German and two Irish.

The earliest known MS is in French and is dated 1371. It has not been printed, but some account of it is given in the Bibliography. A critical French text is urgently needed and has long been contemplated. Nicholson in a letter to *The Academy*, on February 12, 1881, wrote: 'In 1877 I learnt from the French Société de l'Orient Latin that they had in

A full list of all known manuscripts and printed editions is given in Röhricht, *Bibl. Geog. Palaestinae*, 1890, p. 79; and see H. Cordier, *Mélanges*, 1914, vol. 1. Röhricht notes two Irish manuscripts, one Spanish, sixty-five German, two Dutch, two Danish, five Czech, and ten Italian. The Italian MSS have been studied by Vogels, 'Verhältniss der Italienischen version d. Reisebeschreibung Mandeville's zur französischen.' *Festschrift zum Gymnasium Adolfinum zu Mörs*, 1883, p. 37.

hand an elaborate critical text of the original French, which was to have appeared in the autumn of that year, but had been unavoidably deferred.' In 1889 a French edition by Vogels was nearing completion (Warner p. viii), but it was not published. Bovenschen in 1881 (p. 181) speaks of a projected French edition by Michelant, but I can find no further trace of it.

The English text has come down to us, for all practical purposes, in three forms, none older than the fifteenth century, namely Harl. 3954 and others (defective), which have the long gap in the description of Egypt, to which reference has already been made, Cotton MS Titus c. xvi, lacking three leaves, and Egerton 1982. The Cotton MS was the work of a Midland writer. The Egerton MS was the work of a Northerner, who had before him a French, and possibly also the Cotton version, and another English or Latin original. The defective version which was popular in the fifteenth and sixteenth centuries, was much shorter, and the translator was either too dull to note the gap in the French original, or he worked on a defective text. This defective text was the only one printed before 1725. The earliest dated edition was printed by Wynkyn de Worde in 1499 (copies in the University Library, Cambridge, and at Stonyhurst). It was preceded by Pynson's edition, undated, but probably 1496, a unique copy of which is in the Grenville Library. There were fifteen editions in England before 1725, all with the long gap in the description of Egypt, and all based on the defective text. The edition of 1568, printed by East, was reprinted by the Oxford Press in 1936, with the gap filled in from the Cotton MS. East's edition of 1568 contains virtually the same wood-cuts which have been repeated down to the present time.[1]

In 1887, John Ashton reprinted the defective text without taking any notice of the gap, which fills twenty-four pages

[1] Vogels, *Englische Version*, p. 11, is wrong in stating that these illustrations come from Harley 3954. There is in fact no connection.

of the Oxford reprint, although it had already been pointed out by Nicholson and others, with the result that the last line of page 35 makes nonsense. Vogels, who subjected this edition to a slashing attack in 1891, calls it 'blutigen Unsinn,'[1] but we have grown more polite. It is sufficient to say that Ashton professed to find the Cotton version (reprinted by Halliwell in 1839) rude and archaic, and that this indifferent editor complains of his predecessors' lack of care in copying the text. In the Everyman's Library reprint of Ashton's edition the gap has been filled in.

The Cotton version was printed anonymously in 1725. The editor claims that he collated the Cotton text with seven MSS and four old printed editions, but there is little evidence of this. It was reprinted in 1839, with notes and glossary by Halliwell. Until Pollard's edition, Halliwell's edition was the only version of the Cotton MS in print and was for long the standard English text. It was frequently reprinted, but it is not a satisfactory edition. Its defects, which are numerous, have been pointed out by Vogels.[2] In fairness to Halliwell it must be stated that he was only responsible for the notes and glossary.

These reprints follow the earlier text without question, the editors reproducing the capital letters with great care, and leaving the text to look after itself, but they contain the best of the Mandeville stories, and they are important, since it is in this form that Mandeville was first presented to English readers after the invention of printing. This defective version has now been entirely superseded by the Cotton text.

The Cotton version was reprinted in 1900 by A. W. Pollard in Macmillan's 'Library of English Classics,' in modern spelling, but, as might be expected from such a distinguished scholar, the work is most carefully done, without any sacrifice of the spirit or savour of the original.

[1] Vogels, *Englische Version*, p. 5, and see Warner, p. xi, note 3.
[2] Vogels, pp. 8, 9.

It is to my mind the best edition for the general reader. The edition of the Cotton version, printed by Hamelius for the Early English Text Society, with an introduction and valuable notes, will be for many years the standard English text for students, but the editor's claim that the 'Travels' were wholly written by Outremeuse still remains to be substantiated. The Egerton MS was printed for the Roxburghe Club, in 1889, by G. F. (afterwards Sir George) Warner, with a French text based on Harl. 4383, supplemented by Sloane 1464, Royal 20 B.x. and Grenville xxxix (now Add. 33,757). Warner also reproduced twenty-eight fine miniatures from Add. MS 24,189. It is difficult to speak too highly of this scholarly edition, and my debt to it is gratefully acknowledged, the only criticism being that it is scarce and very expensive, and can have reached only a limited public. But Warner has tracked down Mandeville's sources with such deadly effect that only a few pages are left which are not shown to have been stolen. Warner and Bovenschen, between them, have destroyed the last vestiges of any claim to originality. It is an odd circumstance that two scholars, working independently in different countries, should have been engaged on the same task at the same time, and that they should have arrived at the same conclusions. At about this time Dr. Vogels was engaged on his learned enquiries into the sources of the Latin and English manuscripts. The years 1888 to 1891 were indeed memorable years for all students of Mandeville.

As to Latin editions, Vogels records five different renderings. Of the principal version, called by Vogels and Warner the vulgate, there are twelve MSS, none earlier than the fifteenth century, two of which are in the British Museum and one in the Bodleian Library. Of the five versions noted by Vogels, the vulgate alone has been printed (without date or printer's name, but probably about 1484). Of the other versions, seven MSS are in English libraries, and one is at Leyden, and even this was the work of a monk of Abingdon

Abbey, in 1390. The vulgate text was again printed, about 1485, by Gerard Leeu at Antwerp or Gouda (with slight variations), but it has this peculiarity that it contains frequent references to Friar Odoric of Pordenone, whose travels supplied Mandeville with much of his material for the Far East, and whose name was linked with Mandeville's as a possible fellow-traveller. This Antwerp text was the one printed by Hakluyt in the first edition of his 'Voyages,' and reprinted in the edition of 1810, vol. II. Both the vulgate and the Antwerp edition (as we have seen) contain frequent references to the exploits of Ogier the Dane, and these and others were dovetailed into the German translation by Otto von Diemeringen.

Cordier records an edition of von Diemeringen's translation printed in 1475, at Basle, but the British Museum copy is Strasburg, 1484. There was another translation of Michel Velser, or Michel-Felder, as he calls himself, the earliest recorded edition being 1481, Augsburg. The British Museum copy is dated 1482. Both translations have attractive woodcuts. The British Museum also possesses a manuscript of von Diemeringen's translation, Add. MS 17335, with different illustrations (fifteenth century). Velser's translation did not achieve the same popularity as von Diemeringen's which was frequently reprinted and became in time a popular 'Volksbuch.' Both translations have various interesting divergencies and other points of interest and are dealt with elsewhere (p. 135). Bovenschen (p. 81) writes, in 1888, that he had practically completed a study of the German translations, but, like other promised contributions to the Mandeville problem, it failed to appear.

Among other editions it may be noted that there was an Italian edition printed at Milan, 1480, a French edition at Lyons in the same year, a Spanish edition in 1521, while Flemish and Czech editions appeared in 1470 and 1510, respectively.

It is interesting to note that Mandeville's 'Travels' was abridged and reprinted as a chap-book in the eighteenth century. It seems to have been very popular. Several of these chap-books are in the British Museum. Most of the best stories are there, and a few rough woodcuts are added, one edition showing Mandeville in eighteenth-century costume, safe home, with a parrot in one hand and a stick in the other, shooting at an unfortunate blackamore with a blunderbuss, and relating his experiences to a potentate clad in knee breeches. One cannot but admire the skill with which all problems of nationality and date are disposed of. In one edition, by a simple alteration of the date from 1372 to 1732, Mandeville is turned into another Gulliver. His return is related as follows: 'I accordingly set sail for England, and after a very favourable passage, arrived safe on my native shore to the great joy and satisfaction of all my friends. And since my arrival have been employed, by the help of my journals, in compiling this book, which gives an account of what I have seen in my travels, some of which for their strangeness may seem incredible.' The Mappa Mundi appears in other English versions as a map. Here it is turned into a book. 'Those that will not believe the truth of these things, let them but read the book of *Mappa Mundi*, where they will find a great part of it there contained and a good many stranger things than are here recited.' The title-pages are as interesting as the book, and certainly promised good value for the shilling which was charged for it. Here is one of them.

'The Foreign Travels and Dangerous Voyages of the Renowned English Knight Sir John Mandeville, wherein he gives an Account of Remote Kingdoms, Countries, Rivers, Castles, Giants of a prodigious height and strength, the people called Pigmies, very small and of a low stature. To which is added an Account of People of odd deformities: some without heads. Also enchanted wildernesses, where are fiery Dragons, Griffins and many wonderful beasts in the country of Prester John. All very delightful to the reader. Printed and sold in Bow Church Yard.'

And very delightful it must all have been, far more delightful and exciting than 'The History of Charles XII of Sweden', 'The Merry Tales of the Wise Men of Gotham,' and other dull and sober productions which had previously held the field.

CHAPTER XIV

The Cotton and Egerton Versions

SIR GEORGE WARNER'S note on the Cotton manuscript (Cotton Titus. c. xvi) is as follows. 'C. is a small
quarto measuring 8½ inches by 6 inches, with 132 leaves.
The text is written in a neat, well-formed hand, varying
somewhat in parts (more especially at folio 119) but not
enough to make it certain that more than one scribe was
employed. The ornamentation is very simple. There is a
large initial in gold, on a red and blue ground, at the
beginning, and the other initials are in blue, filled in and
flourished with lines in red. The text is divided into
chapters by rubricated titles, without numeration.' The
manuscript has lost a few leaves, which are supplied in
Pollard's and Hamelius' editions from the Egerton version.

According to Vogels the Cotton version, although not
quite complete, is the most original text. Egerton, which is
free from many of the errors in Cotton, he regards as a
composite text, adapting the Cotton version with slight
variations and supplying the gap in the description of
Egypt from an English-Latin version in the Bodleian
Library.[1] This Bodleian English-Latin version presents an
abbreviated and imperfect text, and has not been printed.
Vogels shows, I think conclusively, that this version is
translated from the Latin and not from the French.[2]

The Cotton version, as we have seen, is quite clearly translated from the French. There are a number of gallicisms
which are referred to later, but, apart from these, the true

---

[1] E. Museo, 116 and Rawlinson D. 99.
[2] Vogels, *Englische Version Mandeville's*, p. 46

relationship between the French and English texts is clear from the errors in translation which are dealt with later (p. 145), and which can all be traced back to a French original. But on the whole this unknown translator — a Midlander — did his work well. Even when he succumbed to his weakness for French expressions, these gallicisms do not seriously disfigure the text or deprive it of its English character. The style is vigorous, and the various marvels are related with a plausibility which disarms the reader and carries the story along without apparent effort, and with a minimum of words.

Both Pollard and Warner provide excellent glossaries, and some such help is necessary to-day. In the following notes I have not been so much concerned to look for odd words as to trace the origin of some of the borrowings from the French, an art at which this unknown Englishman was an adept. Such words as *adread* (afraid), *avoutry* (adultery), *clept* (called), *culver* (dove), *quick* (alive) and *sicker* (sure), present no difficulty, but *arboury*, meaning woodland, is unusual and comes direct from the French. The Cotton translator did not apparently even try to find an English equivalent. In the account of the country of Comania, which was either too hot or too cold, the French text has 'poy darbres fruit portantz.' What could be easier than to write: 'In that country is but little arboury ne trees that bear fruit ne other?' Judging by the Oxford English Dictionary the word was quite unusual — only one other (and later) example is given. The Cotton translator was in fact coining a new English word, although it appears to have had no success. Egerton is less ambitious. There the reading is 'few trees that bear fruit.' Another unusual expression, which also comes straight from the French, is *avaled* meaning descended. In the account of Gog and Magog and the Ten Tribes shut up behind the Caspian Mountains by Alexander the Great, the Cotton version reads: 'the Jews have gone up the mountains and availed down to the valleys.' Egerton

XII. ALEXANDER AND THE TREES OF THE SUN
AND THE MOON

From 'The Shrewsbury Book' in the British Museum.

(See p. 97).

XIII. GOLD DIGGING ANTS
From Velser's translation, 1482.
(See p. 98).

XIV ELEPHANT AND PIG
From Velser's translation, 1482.
(See p. 142).

misses the point altogether, and speaks only of climbing the mountains, but the French text has 'ne peut monter ne avaler.' According to the Oxford English Dictionary the word was used by Caxton and Spenser, but no example is given of the use of the word in this sense after 1596.

Another word taken straight from the French is *avoir* meaning riches, which, according to the Oxford English Dictionary, passed into fairly common use as *aver*, signifying possessions, property, farm-stock, cattle and domestic animals of any kind.

Cautels, meaning fraud, has the authority of Bacon, but the Cotton translator got it, as usual, from the French. Writing of Prester John's people, the French text has 'nont cure de barrat ne de cautels, ne de fraudes nulles.' Egerton translates this: 'there is neither with them fraud nor guile.' But Cotton translates literally 'They set not by no barretts, ne by cautels, nor of no deceits.'

Another instance of blind copying from the French occurs in the story of the Castle of the Sparrow-hawk, which was kept by a fair enchantress. Anyone who watched the sparrow-hawk for seven days and nights, without company and without sleep, could have his first wish fulfilled. A king of Armenia, having passed the test, demanded the body of the lady. She said he was a fool to desire what he might not have, for she was not a creature of this earth, but he insisted. Then said this lady: 'Sith that I may not withdraw you from your lewd corage (meaning desire) I shall give you without wishing . . . war without peace' and the king had war to his life's end. The French text has 'vostre fol courage.' Egerton gives 'thy folly.' Cotton takes over the word and is perhaps justified in adding 'lewd,' since one of the definitions in the Oxford English Dictionary is lust or sexual vigour.

Beclippe, which the glossaries explain by 'curdle,' deserves a note to itself. If you took balm from the Balsam Garden at Cairo, you could tell whether it was sophisticate or true by putting a drop into a cup of goat's milk. If the balm was genuine 'anon it will take and beclippe the milk.' Egerton has a still stranger expression, for in that version the milk becomes *leper*, meaning coagulated. The Oxford English Dictionary does not help. It quotes no other use of beclippe, but, as one would expect, it also defines beclippe as 'to fold in the arms, embrace, clasp.' The French text has 'tantot ly lait acoillera et prendra.' *Acoiller* comes from *accueillir* (Latin, *adcolligere*), to join or welcome. It may be that the Cotton translator took the word to mean embrace, and troubled no further, but it is difficult to think of embrace as an equivalent of curdle. The real sense seems to be that the balm mixed with the milk and lost its character. This is confirmed by the Latin text:—*statim miscebit se et unietur cum lacte, ita ut Balsamum non cognoscetur*.

Passing over such expressions as *betook* for 'gave,' *bigged* for 'built,' and *broily* for 'broiled' (the head of St. John Baptist was still to be seen in Rome 'all broilly, as though it were half-burnt') and *buscayle* for 'brushwood,' there is *chamberer* meaning 'concubine': 'And Abraham had another son Ishmael that he gat upon Hagar, his chamberer.' The Oxford English Dictionary under *chamberer*, gives two references only, Mandeville and another, but there can be no doubt as to its origin. It comes from the French: 'Agar, sa chambrere.' The Italian version (Milan 1480) follows suit with 'Ager, sua camerera,' and Egerton omits it altogether. It is intersting to note that, while the Cotton translator could make good use of his French original, he could at times shoot very wide of the mark. Instances of mistranslation are given later (p. 145). Another one occurs in the strange description of the garden of transmigrated souls in the abbey near the city of Cassay. In this abbey was a fair garden, in which were 'apes, marmosets, baboons and many other diverse beasts.' The fair beasts were the souls of worthy men, but the foul beasts were the souls of poor men and of rude commons. Every day after dinner a monk rang a silver bell, and the creatures came down to eat what was left over from the meal. The French text is quite clear: 'et sonne une clokette d'argent.' Egerton has 'a little bell of silver,' and the Italian version reads 'fa sonare una campanela dargento.' The Cotton version, on the other hand, has: 'And every day, when the convent of this abbey hath eaten, the almoner . . . smiteth on the garden gate with a clicket of silver,' clicket signifying a kind of latch-key. The smiting on the garden gate is Cotton's own invention. He obviously misunderstood the whole passage.

Forcelets (for castles) comes from the French *forceresses* or *forteresses*. *Galaoth* (a helmet) is a direct transfer from the French *galahoth* (Egerton has hat), but one other transfer deserves special mention. In the description of the entertainments provided by jugglers and magicians at the Great Chan's court, we are told that knights appeared by magic and jousted in the air, running together 'a great random, and they frussch together full fiercely, and they break their spears so rudely that the truncheons fly in sprouts and pieces all about the hall.' *Frussch*, a most expressive word, appears, to us at least, to lose force in the French *froissent*. Egerton's translator, although he heightens the atmosphere of magic, is also rather tame with 'smite so samen with their spears.' 'Jonks of the sea,' from which the thorns of the Crown of Thorns were taken, comes from the *iouncs marinz*. *Destrier*, a war horse, is both French and English, although Egerton has 'a great steed or hier.' *Ere*, to plough, is taken over from the French *arer*. In the Valley Perilous (see above, p. 88) the *nakers* or drums, which frightened the travellers so badly, have a good French original in *nakairez* or *nacaires*, but the word seems to have had no currency here after the fourteenth century. *Swevenes* (dreams) is the Cotton translation of *mauvais signes de visions*, and other examples are given under *sweven* in the Oxford English Dictionary. *Gabbers*, for 'cheats,' was used by Chaucer (Fr. *barratours*) and *grucched* (for complaint) has a fairly respectable history and gave us 'grudged.' The word occurs in the account of the passage of the Children of Israel through the desert, when they *grucched* because there was no water. The Egerton version is far less forceful with 'made murmuration,' but is closer to the French text, *murmuroit*.

I conclude this survey of the Cotton translation with a strange use of the word *skill*, and with two other direct borrowings from the French. In the account of the lords and other people of Cyprus, we are told that, by reason of the great heat, they dug trenches in the earth, deep to the knee, so that they could sit there and take their meals in comfort. The *skill*, or reason, was that 'they may be the more fresh.' Egerton follows the French text 'Qar ceo est la guise par de la pur estre pluis freschement,' almost literally with 'This is the cause for to be more fresh,' but *skill* (for reason, or cause) seems to have been fairly common down to the seventeenth century, and is used in this sense by Shakespeare in 'The Winter's Tale.' The two French transfers are *fertre* and *enombred*. The first occurs in the description of the monastery of St. Catherine at Mount Sinai, where the saint's body lay in a *fertre* or bier (French, *fiertre*). No other use of this word in English seems to be known. The other is a curious expression which can best be explained in its context. We are told that when God was made man he was *enombred* in the Virgin Mary. Egerton has 'lighted in the Virgin Mary,' although it is interesting to note that Egerton uses the word *oumbre* elsewhere for shadow. Cotton's word comes from the French *enombra*. Pollard gives the meaning as shadow or shroud, which is perhaps as good as any other, although *incarnate* (from the Latin version) might be better. The word does not appear in the Oxford English Dictionary.

The Egerton version is perhaps the more original in style. It omits many of the errors and gallicisms into which the Cotton translator fell, and it is at times more personal. It does not adhere as closely to the French text as Cotton, and at times it gives the impression of being a paraphrase rather than a translation. The more emphatic 'I' is apparent here and there, and the comparisons are often very vivid. The proper names are less confused and, if only on philological grounds, it deserves a place by itself, but, as it has only been printed for the Roxburghe Club, it cannot be expected to reach a wide public until it has been modernised, and this presents considerable difficulties.

The Egerton version is the work of a Northerner, and there are plenty of northern and unfamiliar words. Sir George Warner describes the manuscript (Egerton MS 1982) as of exactly the same measurements as the Cotton MS, but the leaves (129 in number) have been sheared for binding. 'The hand is a little firmer and bolder, and is manifestly the same throughout. The ornamentation is still more severe, the large initial at the beginning, otherwise closely resembling that in C., not being gilded (though apparently intended to be) and the smaller red and blue initials being perfectly plain, without flourishes. The text is not divided into chapters, but the names of places, etc., are frequently noted in the margin, some of them being in Latin.'

There is an inscription on a fly-leaf which Sir George Warner reproduces as it stands:— 'On a leaf of paper pasted on the inside of the ancient cover of this MSS (sic), and too friable and decayed to be separated from it and preserved, there was written: *Thys fayre Boke I have fro the abbey at Saint Albons in thys year of our Lord M.CCCCLXXXX the sixt daye of Apryl. Willyam Caxton — Richard Tottyl, 1579 — Lond. This Book was given to me by the Revd. Hugh Tuthill, a descendant of the above named Richard Tottyl, who was a celebrated Printer —* E. Hill, M.D., March 22d. 1803.' As Sir George Warner observes, one would like to think that the MS passed through Caxton's hands, but there is nothing to show that Caxton or Tottel printed a Mandeville.

The first to draw attention to the Egerton version was E. W. B. Nicholson, who mentions it in a letter to *the*

Academy dated 11 November, 1876. The north-country expressions give this version a pleasant and homely flavour. The bitter water healed by Elisha at Jericho becomes a *beck* running between the hills, *Ilk*, *mickle* and *kirk* appear on nearly every page. *Childer* is used for children. In the passage describing the Greek Church the word *oker* appears for usury ('They say that oker is no deadly sin'). One of the difficulties in modernising this text is the use of the word *ger — gert* (cause or caused). It appears constantly — 'he will ger cry out in the middle of a town.' 'St. John gert make his grave there [at Ephesus] in his life and laid himself therein all quick.' 'This emperor gert enclose the kirk of the sepulchre with a wall, and made it to be within the city, that before was without,' and so on. Nor is the task of modernisation rendered easier by the use of *warne* (unless), *buse* (must), *beese* (is), *tome* (empty), *umgwhyle* (formerly), *sammen* (together), *almous gerne* (charitable), *bowsoumness* (obedience), *miste* (need), *motyng* (debate), *sawghtling* (agreement), *umgang* (circuit), or *ferrum* (from afar). In the description of the Balsam Garden at Cairo, Cotton has: 'Men cut the branches with a sharp flintstone.' Egerton writes 'That instrument is called gaylounagon.' One has to go to the French *cailou aigu* before one can even get a glimpse of what was in the translator's mind. *Syde* (long) is another difficulty: 'In another isle are folk whose ears are so syde that they hang down to the knees.'

I deal later with some of the errors in translation in both Cotton and Egerton, but enough has been said to show that the Egerton version — attractive and interesting as it is — is not likely to displace the Cotton text, so far as the general reader is concerned.

CHAPTER XV

The German Translations

(a) VON DIEMERINGEN'S TRANSLATION

THE French, Italian and Spanish translations do not call for special mention, but the German translations have an interest of their own. Von Diemeringen's translation was the subject of a slashing attack by J. J. von Görres, in 1807.[1] He complains that von Diemeringen often completely misunderstood his text, that place names are corrupt, and that the whole book is confused. There is some justification for this, but perhaps the crowning absurdity is the transformation (at times, but not always) of the Grand Can into the Great Dog (*der grosse Hund*).

Von Diemeringen tells us that he translated from Latin and French, but the frequent references to Ogier the Dane make it clear that he must have used some text, at present unidentified, which passed through Outremeuse's hands.[2] Another interesting feature is the presence of eight alphabets. No other version known to me has as many, but I will deal with this problem later. There is a manuscript version (15th century) of this translation at the British Museum,[3] but, so far as I can judge, except for the illustrations, there is no important variation from the printed text.

Despite its defects, von Diemeringen's translation is lively and readable, and the woodcuts (of the Alsace School, coloured by hand in the British Museum copy of the 1484 edition) are excellent of their kind. The concluding note is interesting as showing the popularity of Mandeville's book

[1] *Die Teutschen Volksbücher*, p. 53.   [2] See above p. 114.   [3] Add. MS 17335.

in the great European trading centres. After speaking of the merchants of Paris, Bruges and England who had seen God's wonders for themselves and visited many lands, von Diemeringen declares that knights, merchants and pilgrims had all confirmed the truth of the narrative and that, at the instance of merchants resorting to Bruges, he had turned the book from Latin and French into German. One curious feature is that the chapters on the customs of the Saracens and their law, and on the life of Mahomet, which in most versions are found in the early part of the book, are relegated to the end, and that Mandeville's curious colloquy with the Sultan is omitted altogether. The translation is divided into books and chapters, and there is a detailed summary of contents at the end. The book was evidently carefully prepared for the press. That Mandeville was popular in Germany is clear from the fact that out of some 300 manuscripts known to exist, sixty-five are in German.

It would take too long to describe the variations between this most interesting and lively version and the other texts as we have them, but some of the changes deserve special notice. We learn that Mount Ararat was several miles high and that Mandeville would have gone up himself, if it had not been the month of August and too hot. He relates the story of the monk who climbed up and brought down the plank from the Ark which was preserved in the monastery at the foot of the mountain. In the German translation, but not in other versions, Mandeville claims to have seen it with his own eyes. We learn, too, that when Noah came down from Mount Ararat he built two cities, one called Landarie and the other Herma in which were 1000 churches. The Cotton version calls the towns Dain and Any. There is a curious addition to the story of the Amazons, not in any other version known to me. Apparently the Amazon queen had her own views about religion. She inclined to the doctrine of anti-Christ and liked to hear sermons on the subject. There is a fine picture of the queen wearing her crown and listening to a preacher declaiming from a box-like pulpit, while a gentleman-at-arms stands by, and behind the queen is a lady-in-waiting wearing a wimple. We learn, too, that the Amazons did many doughty deeds in battle against the Greeks and Hercules, and that they had a man's courage without his arrogance.

Before the description of India, the More, the Less and Middle India, there is a dissertation (which may well be a gloss by von Diemeringen himself, who was a cleric) on God's wonders and the danger of disbelieving travellers' tales because they were strange. It must be remembered that God, who made Heaven and Earth with one word, was able in his power and might to create men, women and beasts of all shapes and diverse natures. India was so called from the river Ind. It was largely composed of islands, some more than 5000 miles in extent, each with stately towns and noble castles. The people were all yellow, as if they suffered from jaundice. The country was unknown to us, partly because the people did not visit other lands, preferring to stay in their country — hot as it was — rather than to change it for a worse. Another reason was that there were murderous and savage beasts by the way, steep precipices, overhanging rocks and raging seas, in which many persons had perished. Nevertheless, merchants from Venice, Genoa and other places were found there, buying and selling merchandise, and behaving as merchants will all the world over.

As to the Ogier stories, as I have already indicated, this version marks stage three in the development of Outremeuse's connection with the 'Travels' and contains more Ogier references than any of the versions known to me (above p. 114).

There are two Ogier references in the first part of the 'Travels' (Bk. I, ch. XXIX, XLII), both of which can be traced to the *Myreur* — the campaign against the Bedouins, in which Ogier was of course triumphant, and the capture or building of the castle of Montroyal, south of the Dead Sea

(*Myreur*, III, pp. 54, 55). But they need not detain us long. Ogier's outstanding triumphs were in the East.

India was, so to speak, a different world from ours, for it was entirely surrounded by mountains, and, if one found the entrance, there were other mountains beyond so close together that the people on one mountain could hear the people talking on the other. That was when the sea dividing them was calm. During storms no ships could live there, and the people were completely cut off from each other. Few travellers could find their way thither on account of the danger of the route, but the rulers of Babylonia, Alexandria and the Romans had made a road from Persia. It was Ogier who, with the help of the Genoese and Venetians, Prester John and the Great Chan who improved it, so that it was passable on that side. This story is not in any other version of Mandeville known to me, and there is no corresponding reference in the *Myreur*.

It was Ogier again who founded the towns of Flandrine and Florence in the land of Lomb, and named them after his grandmother Flandrina and his mother Florentina. (A long disquisition follows on Ogier's ancestry). Christians and Jews lived there together in amity, for it was a good land, although very hot. Many Christians lived also in Sarche, where Ogier had built churches for them. The *Myreur* (III, p. 57) gives an abbreviated account, but says that the two towns were named after '*la mère de son père et la mère de sa mère.*'

Von Diemeringen also adds the interesting information that the trees bearing meal, honey and venom were named after Ogier. With the venom the Jews had tried to destroy all Christians, but thanks to Almighty God the plot failed. The other trees had been provided by God so that Ogier and his host might have food. No man knew of their virtue until an angel showed them to Ogier; they were still called Ogier's trees, and the fruit was called Ogier's fruit.

Von Diemeringen's account of the miracle of the fishes

is also new. It will be recalled that great quantities of fish cast themselves up on the sea-shore in the isle of Calonak, where they remained for three days, so that the men of that country might take as many as they liked. Then the survivors swam away and others took their place. So great was the press that it seemed as if the fish were drawn by some hidden bait. The real explanation was to be found in a certain Book of Chronicles. When Ogier and his host were famished, God ordained that the fish should offer themselves for food, for Ogier was God's champion.

Both these stories are in the *Myreur*, III, p. 62. When besieging the city of Agrippaige, Ogier's army suffered from famine. The adjoining isle of Orquebans was then shown to Ogier with trees bearing meal, honey, wine and venom, after which he captured the city. Further details are added in the manuscript summarized by Michel (above, p. 109) which may well have a fuller version, placing the fish before the trees. The angel is mentioned, but the fish were provided for the army's Lenten fare, and the famine was a punishment for the soldiers' neglect of Lent, which seems a little hard under all the circumstances. Von Diemeringen's mention of a Book of Chronicles is interesting, if, as I think, von Diemeringen was translating from a text in which Outremeuse had inserted the Ogier references. Outremeuse was once again pushing his own book.

Von Diemeringen tells the usual story about the dooms or judgments pronounced by the hand of St. Thomas in the church at Mabaron. He adds, however, another account, based on a book by St. Gregory,[1] of how the saint's hand administered the sacrament to the faithful, but withheld it from sinners and heretics, which agrees in many particulars with the story as related in one of the documents associated with Prester John's Letter (above, p. 59), and which I have not found in any other version of Mandeville. The *Myreur*

[1] Gregory of Tours, *Lib. Mirac*, cap. 32.

gives only the usual account of the dooms pronounced by the saint's hand (III, pp. 58, 59).

As we have seen, the palace of the King of Java was adorned with pictures of Ogier's exploits. The Latin vulgate text relates this briefly, but von Diemeringen gives it in greater detail. He tells us how Ogier came from France and conquered all lands from Rome to India, how the goddess Jana made him immortal. How, after 200 years, he returned to France, thinking that he had only been absent for one year, and how he marvelled to find so much changed in one year, for no one knew him. There were pictures also of Hector, Alexander, Hercules and Charlemagne, but their deeds were not comparable with Ogier's, for he subdued all who were not Christians from sunrising to sunsetting. Even, to this day, the rulers of India were descended from his line. The pictures told how Ogier was taken prisoner by Charlemagne and kept at Mecca, but, when King Josore attacked France, the emperor set Ogier free to fight against that king. Ogier slew Josore before Lâon, then marched against the heathen, according to a vow taken in prison. When he came to the country of King Josore's father, called Bereiher, that king made a treaty with the Templars to betray Ogier to him, but the plot failed, and Ogier conquered his country and all other heathen lands. He called himself God's soldier, for he fought not for land or dominion, but only to convert the heathen. It was said that Ogier still lives and will come again to set all countries to rights.

The pictures of Ogier's exploits are not described in the *Myreur* for obvious reasons. They could not be there until after his time, but it is interesting to compare von Diemeringen's account with the events as described in the *Myreur*, if only to see how skilfully the various episodes were transferred from the *Myreur* to Mandeville's text. The events related in the *Myreur* are as follows: Ogier is embroiled by the traitor Ganelon with Charlemagne after

Ogier's return from his first voyage to the East, and the breach becomes open when (III, p. 194) Charlemagne's bastard son, Charlot, kills Ogier's bastard son Bauduinet. Ogier sails a second time for the East (III, p. 258), saves Constantinople from the Saracens and sets out for India, but is driven back by a storm and wrecked at Genoa. On 4 February, 838, he is taken prisoner by Turpin at Yvorie in Savoy (III, p. 268) and transferred to Rheims, where Charlemagne sets him free (III, p. 289), and Ogier defeats the Saracens before Lâon by decapitating their king, Bréhier (III, p. 300). On his third visit to the East he cleans up Rhodes, where Christian princes were meditating apostasy to Mahomet (III, p. 318–320; A.D. 850). On his fourth visit to the East (III, p. 337–374; A.D. 857) he captures Acre, but is betrayed by the Templars to Ysoré, king of the Saracens. He is later taken to Mecca (III, p. 345). He escapes, retakes Acre and hangs the guilty Templars. It is Morgan la Fay, not the Goddess Jana, who makes Ogier immortal. On his fifth and last visit to the East to recapture Acre (IV p. 41–145) in A.D. 895, when Ogier is in his 97th year, he stays at Avalon with King Arthur and Morgan la Fay. He is rejuvenated and has children by Morgan. On his return to France he falls into decrepitude, becomes a monk, and, when about to die, is carried off again (IV, p. 138) by Morgan to Avalon, where he lives in eternal youth to this day. He returns in 1214 to help the French under Philip Augustus at the battle of Bouvines (V. p. 144).

As will be seen, practically the whole of this is summarized by von Diemeringen. He gives other Ogier stories, e.g. that the women in the kingdom of Mancy still wore a horned headdress in memory of Ogier (*Myreur*, III, p. 63), and that the name Prester John was bestowed on that potentate by Ogier when he gave him his kingdom; but enough has been said to show that von Diemeringen must have been working on a MS which can be traced back to

Outremeuse. His hand is apparent throughout. It would require little more to make Ogier the hero of the 'Travels' instead of Mandeville.

Von Diemeringen has many references to Alexander the Great, two of which are new to me. It was well known that elephants could not abide pigs. When Alexander was fighting in India he used pigs successfully against the elephants of the king of Calonach. What was not well known was that pigs could not abide the smell of burnt feathers. When therefore the Indians used pigs against Alexander's elephants, he gathered together all the hens he could find, had their feathers singed, and drove them among the pigs, whereupon they fled in disorder, and Alexander's elephants marched to victory (Bk. II, ch. XIII). The other story concerns Alexander's approach to the walls of Paradise. When he arrived he found the premises closed for the time being. Realizing that there were limits to his conquests, he set up two columns on a lofty mountain towards sunrising (finely pictured by von Diemeringen's artist), just as Hercules set up his pillars in the Spanish sea towards sunsetting, as a sign that no one could go beyond them. They were called Alexander's Gades (Bk. IV, ch. XIII).[1]

The story has its sequel in the travels of Marignolli, who visited the court of the Great Chan as papal legate in the fourteenth century,[2] for he claims to have gone beyond Alexander's columns and to have set up his own landmark there. 'For I erected a stone as my landmark and memorial in the corner of the world over against Paradise, and anointed it with oil. In sooth it was a marble pillar with a stone cross upon it, intended to last till the world's end. And it had the Pope's arms and my own engraved upon it, with inscriptions both in Latin and Indian characters. I consecrated and blessed it in the presence of an infinite

---

[1] The Pillars of Hercules were called *Gades Herculis*, and are so named in the Hereford Map. "Gades" seems to come from Cadiz and was the equivalent of columns. Bevan and Phillott, *Med. Geography*, 1873, p. 112.

[2] Yule, *Cathay*, III, p. 218.

multitude of people, and I was carried on the shoulders of the chiefs in a litter or palankin like Solomon's.' Marignolli's landmark was not destined to last until the world's end, but a Dutch chaplain claims to have seen it in 1662, after which it is believed to have been washed away.

(b) VELSER'S TRANSLATION

Velser's translation was first printed in Augsburg, in 1481, by Anton Sorg. The British Museum copy is dated 1482. This translation is much more direct and business-like than von Diemeringen's. Velser worked apparently on a good French text. There are no Ogier references, but Velser adds a personal note here and there, as if to justify the marvels he has to set down. In dealing with the artificial incubation of chickens at Cairo, he remarks that no one should doubt the truth of such stories, as he himself had seen a dog which had been hatched out of a clutch of three birds' eggs, and he gives a fine picture of the bird with a puppy emerging from an egg. Again, when he comes to the description of the Great Chan's court, he adds a note: 'I Michelfelder, who translated this book into German, had speech with a worthy person named Saraphel, who was eighteen years in distant parts with his master. He told me that he had seen the Great Chan out hunting and that he had 200,000 men in attendance.' Velser found the adventures in the Valley Perilous (above p. 91) almost beyond belief, and his description of what happened there is printed at the end of chapter IX.

Velser's illustrations are not as spirited as von Diemeringen's, but there are some fine pictures of monsters. It is interesting to note that Velser relates the story of the elephants and the pigs as given by von Diemeringen, and gives a picture of a pig about to run between an elephant's legs, but says nothing about Alexander the Great, or the use of burnt feathers to drive away the pigs. The translation,

with some additions from von Diemeringen, was modernised and reprinted by Simrock in *Die deutschen Volksbücher*,
1867, Vol XIII.

I (*a*) Saracen, a–m, from Brussels 10420.

(*b*) Saracen, a–m. from Bib. Nat. 4515.

(*c*) Hebrew, a–f, from von Diemeringen, 1484.

(*d*) Runic, a–g, from a MS of Hrabanus Maurus.
(Comparison shows that [*a*], [*b*], and [*c*] are derived from [*d*]).

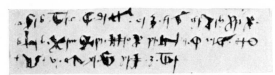

II. Cathayan, t–z, from von Diemeringen, 1484.

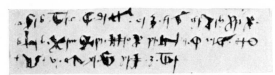

III. Pentexoire, complete, from Brussels 10420. (Comparison of last line with von Diemeringen's Cathayan shows that these two alphabets are doublets. See p. 145).

XV. ALPHABETS
(See ch. XVII).

ye first a lytel Cytee laÿge and narowe and
rÿȝt And wel ÿ walled and enclosed Wiÿ a dÿche
and hit was ÿ Wonede to be called. Effratta
as holÿ Wryte seyþe

 þat ys to say. loo Wee herde hym
yn ye Effratu toWarde ye ende of ye Cytee.
toWarde ye Efte ys a rÿȝt fayre chirche and
a gracious and hÿt haþe manÿ toWres pÿna
cles and kÿrnelles ful strangelÿ ÿ made and
Wiÿ yn þat churche ys xliiÿ. pÿlleres of aʒar
bre. grett and fayre. And bÿ tWÿne þat ylke
churche. and ye Cytee ys ye feelde florÿdoms
and hit ye callede ye feelde ÿ floresthede ffor

also mochel as a fayre maÿden þat was bla
mede Wiÿ Wronge þat sthee hadde ÿ doon for
nÿcacion. ffor ye Whÿche cause sthee was de
mede to ye Deye. and to be beruede yn þat pla
ce to ye Whÿche sthe was ÿ ladde. and as ye
Woode began to breme a bonte hure sthee

made hure prayers tyl oure lord as sthee
was not gÿltÿ of þat ylke þyng þat he Wol
de helpe hure þat hyt mÿȝt ben kloWen to
alle maner of men and Wymmen and sthee
hadde þus seyde sthe entred yn to ye fyre.

And also sone was ye fyre oute. And ye bra
ches þat Were bremÿnge be come rede rose
res. And yees branches þat Were nouȝt ÿ
kendelede. be come Whÿte roseres ful of ro
fes. And yees Were ye fyrfte roseres and ro

fes. þat ene enÿ man saWe And þus was ye

XVI. FROM A MANDEVILLE MS IN THE BRITISH
MUSEUM

CHAPTER XVI

The Transformation of Place-Names
and Errors in Translation

WITH a popular work such as Mandeville, of which at least 300 MSS have survived, with translations into every European language, it is obvious that copyists and translators must have erred at times through lack of attention or fatigue, or from a complete misunderstanding of the original text. Many of these errors are instructive, all are amusing, and some have a real bearing on the development of the various translations.

To deal first with place-names. In the opening pages of the Cotton version, in which the author describes the way to Constantinople, we have the following: 'Men pass through the land of Pyncemartz and come to Greece to the city of Nye, and to the city of Fynepape, and after to the city of Dandrenoble.' (Dandrenoble is of course d'Adrianople, the translator having mistaken the preposition d' for the initial letter of the name). The Egerton version has much the same, but adds 'Sternes and to the city of Affynpayn.' Sternes is Hesternit or Sofia, and appears as Sternez in the history of the First Crusade by Albert of Aix. Fynepape is Philippopolis, called Finopolis or Phinepopolis in the Middle Ages. The earliest French text of 1371 has 'Finepape,' so that no blame attaches to the Cotton translator. Other French texts have much the same, although one version, Sloane 560 (fifteenth century), has 'a la citee de Sternes et puis affyn. Eppape,' and when we come to the Latin versions the confusion is extraordinary. The Latin vulgate text (c. 1484) has 'Asmepape.' Among other Latin MS versions, Ashmole 679 (Bodleian, c. 1450) has Synopapo. Harl. 82 (fifteenth century) has 'Finipapam.' A Latin MS at Leyden dated 1390 (Vulcanii, 96) and Egerton 672 (fifteenth-century) have 'ad fines Epapie,' the Latin translator having turned the first syllable into 'fines' and discovered an unknown country called 'Epapia.' The German version of Michel Velser (1482 ed.) has 'Asmopappe,' which suggests a Latin original (although he says that he translated from the French), but von Diemeringen (1484 ed.) gives 'Synape,' which goes straight back to the French texts, the f being mistaken for a long s. The Italian edition of 1480 has 'Astines.' The English printed version in use down to 1725, when the Cotton version was first printed, has 'Affinpane,' which also suggests a Latin original.

The name Pyncemartz in Cotton (Pynceras in Egerton) — the land of the Pincenati, south of the Danube — mentioned just before Fynepape, seems also to have caused a certain amount of confusion. The French text of 1371 has 'Pintenars,' and this appears to have been followed fairly closely until we come to the German versions, where it appears as 'Pigmeger-lande' (v. Diemeringen)[1] and 'Pinferas' (Velser). But the Italian printed edition of 1480 strikes out an entirely fresh line with 'Prontenardi.' Even stranger is the transformation in chapter 1 of the name Malaville, the modern Semlin, near Sofia. The French text of 1371 has Maleville, but other French texts add the article 'la.' Egerton omits it altogether, and both the German translators leave it alone. It was reserved for the Cotton translator to settle the matter. He calls it 'the evil town.' Other fifteenth century texts give the same reading, but a MS at the British Museum of the fifteenth century (Royal 17.C.xxxviii) gives 'the same town,' the copyist, probably a northerner, having

---

[1] v. Diemeringen's name suggests the pigmy-country. He describes the pigmies, *pigmeer*, in Bk. 3, ch. xix. He may have thought that the Danube was on the borders of that strange country, although a Canon of Metz ought to have known better.

obviously misread 'ilc' for 'ile'.[1] The earliest printed English version has 'yle torne,' another copyist has 'yll Torwe,' and two MSS quoted by Vogels give 'a great toun,' while a French MS of the fifteenth century (Harl. 204) breaks new ground with 'la meliour ville.'

In his account of Cyprus the Cotton translator (ch. v) speaks of 'the castle of Amours', where lay the body of St. Hilarion. This was the castellum Didymus, now known as St. Hilarion, and the transition from Didymus to Amours has a curious history. The German knight Boldensele, from whom Mandeville was now copying, has Gedamoros (Damoros). A Brussels MS of the late fifteenth century (Bibl. Royale 10420) has 'et en castial de damars,' but the French text of 1371 gives 'chastel damours.' This is followed by the Leyden MS (1390) referred to above, which has 'in castello amoris,' although the Latin vulgate edition of c. 1484 prints 'in castro Damers.' The German Velser has ‚ein castel dz heist domonis,' while von Diemeringen goes completely off the rails with 'Dendomones.' The Italian printed edition of 1480 has 'nel castelo damore.'

Another strange slip occurs in chapter v of the Cotton translation. Here the story is told of the young man who visited and desecrated the tomb of his dead lady-love. After nine months, when he again visited the tomb, there flew out an edder [adder] right hideous to see, which destroyed the city. Egerton has 'a head right horrible and hideous to see.' The French text of 1371 has 'teste.' The Italian printed version of 1480 has 'una testa bruta,' and the German translations both have 'Haupt,' but one French MS (Brussels 10420) has 'bieste.' It would seem that the Cotton translator misread 'bieste' for 'teste,' or that he worked on a text in which the word 'bieste' occurred, and turned it into a snake.

In chapter xi the Cotton version relates how Charlemagne brought the preputium of Christ from Jerusalem 'to

Paris into his chapel,' and then to 'Peyteres & Chartres.'
Egerton follows suit. This provides an interesting example
of the dangers which can overtake unwary translators. The
earliest French text of 1371 has 'il le porta a ays la chappelle
. . . et puis a poitiers et . . . a chartres.' The reference to Ays
is of course to Aix-la-chapelle. But this was too much for the
Cotton translator. Chapelle was clear enough, but he could
only make a wild guess at Ayes, which he turned into Paris,
Paris being mentioned in chapter 11 as the place where part
of the Crown of Thorns was to be seen. No German translator, however, was likely to make such a mistake. Velser
omits the passage, as does the Latin vulgate edition —
which again suggests that Velser had access to a Latin
version; but von Diemeringen, as might be expected, prints
'Aachen' and adds 'in unser frawen kirchen.'

In chapter xxxiv of the Cotton version the story is related of the rich Chinaman who was waited upon by fifty
maidens, and whose nails were so long that he could not
feed himself. In his garden was a little mountain where there
was a little meadow, and in that meadow was 'a little toothill,' with towers and pinnacles of gold. Egerton has merely
'a little hill.' The French text of 1371 has 'en mylieu du
jardin il y a un petit moustier' [minster] and other texts
follow pretty closely. The Latin vulgate edition has 'aedi-
ficio, quasi ad scema nostrarum ecclesiarum.' Velser translates simply 'ein münstre.' Von Diemeringen has 'ein clines
münsterlin.' Toothill is defined in the O.E.D. as a natural
or artificial hill or mound, and one can only assume that the
Cotton translator (and to some extent the Egerton translator) had misread 'moustier' for 'montoir,' meaning a hill
or mount;[1] but toothill is a delightful and unexpected
changeling, one of those pleasant surprises which remind
us once again that the Cotton version, with all its faults, is
not only a masterpiece of translation but a landmark in
English literature.

[1] See Hamelius' ed. II, p. 114, for a similar use of *montoir*.

Other errors in translation were long ago pointed out by Sir George Warner. Two are almost commonplaces by this time: 'nonains cordelières,' translated as 'nuns of an hundred orders,' the Englisher having misread 'c' as the numeral 100, and 'swans of heaven' for 'signes du ciel' (signs of the Zodiac) — the translator having taken 'signes' for 'cygnes.' Any student of early manuscripts will realize how easily the Danube could become damby or dammby or even danmby. Nor was the Cotton translator much to blame for turning 'cheminées d'enfer' into 'chemins d'enfer,' which he translates as 'the ways of hell.' Of Samaria (chapter XII) the same translator says that 'it sits between the hill of Aygnes as Jerusalem doth,' which is of course stark nonsense, but it may well be that in the French original 'et siet entre montaignes' the word mont-aignes was so divided at the end of a line, and that the translator mistook the second syllable for a proper name. A statement in chapter VIII of the Egerton version shows that this translator, although he avoids a good many of Cotton's slips, could also misunderstand his text. It is related there that in the deserts of Arabia it behoved travellers to have men with them who could speak Latin, an assertion which simply does not make sense, until we realize that the French word is 'latiniers' or 'latimiers' meaning interpreters. Cotton avoids this slip and writes 'latymers' — 'latiners' in Pollard.

But Egerton's strangest blunder is his 'salt catte.' We read that when Lot's wife looked back to the burning cities she was turned into a 'salt catte,' a reading which gave Sir George Warner much food for thought, although he himself suggested the true solution. The Cotton version (chapter XII) follows the French text of 1371 'pierre de seil' with 'in likeness of a salt stone.' Velser has 'verwandelt in ein salcz saul,' and adds 'et versa est in statuam salis.' Von Diemeringen has 'verwandelt in ein stein.' No one else in short seems to have been at a loss. The mistake arose, without doubt, from a confusion between 'statuam salis' (with a

long s)[1] and 'statuam felis,' although this presupposes that
the Egerton translator had by him a Latin text which has
already been suggested by Vogels.[2] I have referred to three
MS Latin versions at the British Museum, all of the fifteenth
century, Egerton 672, Harley 82 & Royal 13.E.ix. Egerton
672 has 'in statuam salis conversa,' Harley 82 has 'in petram
salis conversa,' and Royal 13 E.ix has 'in statuam lapideam
conversa, seu petram salis.' Only Harley 82 has the long s,
and here 'salis' is in fact not unlike 'felis' — a bad 'a' and
the mischief is done.

[1] The words come from the Vulgate O.T., Genesis, XIX, 26, 'versa est in
statuam salis.'
[2] *Englische Version*, p. 51.

The Alphabets*

SCATTERED at intervals through the text of Mandeville's 'Travels' are a number of enigmatic alphabets,
one for each of the more important countries which he
describes. They consist normally of the forms of the letters,
their names, and key letters, showing to which letter of the
modern European alphabet each form corresponds. They
range from genuine Greek, through unrecognisably corrupt Egyptian, Hebrew, Saracen, Persian, Chaldean,
Tartar-Russ and Cathayan, to an incredible production
called Pentexoire, the language of Prester John's empire.
The names of the letters do not vary significantly from the
earliest to the latest MSS, a word being less vulnerable than
a hieroglyph to a tired or careless scribe. The forms, however, are, even in the best MSS hitherto available to
scholars, already hopelessly corrupt, until in the later MSS
they degenerate rapidly and are finally omitted altogether,
being too obviously debased to be worth reproducing. The
forms are absent in all the seven Latin MSS seen by us, and
from all printed editions so far available in any language,[1]
except those of von Diemeringen's German translation.

The alphabets have been despaired of by former com-
mentators. Warner says that they are 'too corrupt to be
worth reproducing.' Hamelius (in his edition of the Cotton
version, vol. II, p. 22) suspects them to be a set of codes

---

* This chapter is the joint work of the author and Mr. G. D. Painter.

[1] To mention only those texts which were printed before 1600, we have examined
four Latin editions, two French, two English, two Dutch, twenty-one Italian, three
Spanish and one German other than that of von Diemeringen, none of which
contain alphabets complete with forms.

for the use of opponents of the papacy. He admits the objection that, if this were so, we would expect to find documents in these characters, and that no such documents are known. An examination of the alphabets in nearly thirty MSS and printed sources indicates a graver objection. The medieval scribe found such difficulty in copying these unfamiliar hieroglyphs, that every reproduction differs from every other, always considerably and often so widely that only prolonged analysis can establish the connection. In consequence, an anti-papist using an alphabet from one MS would be totally unintelligible to his friend using the corresponding alphabet from another. The possibility remains that the alphabets were fabrications; but we hope to show that those which we shall call the alphabets of the 'first family,' were copied by the author of the 'Travels,' like the remainder of his compilation, from the best available sources. The author may have thought that the alphabets would be of use to travellers, but more probably they were introduced in order to increase the atmosphere of wonder and mystery which surrounds the whole book. If this was his aim it was certainly successful, for the scribes, with their strange hieroglyphics, produced something far more likely to mystify the reader than any pictorial artist, however skilful, could hope to do. Still the fact remains that the writers of medieval guide books did include alphabets for the convenience of travellers, as did, in succeeding centuries, Breydenbach and von Harff. The difference is that Breydenbach and von Harff collected theirs on the spot, while Mandeville (possible as it is that he actually travelled in the Near East) relied on previous authorities for alphabets, as indeed for nearly everything else.

The canon of the alphabets is divisible into two families of MSS.

I. contains, when complete, Greek, Egyptian, Hebrew, Saracen, Persian and Chaldean.

II. Not previously noticed by editors, includes the alphabets in I and adds Tartar-Russ, Cathayan and Pentexoire.

The only good copy of the first family is contained in the Paris MS Bib. Nat. Nouv. acq. franç. 4515, but it occurs frequently elsewhere and is to be found in some form in eight of the ten French MSS, and in seven of the nine English MSS of Mandeville in the British Museum, all the MSS in fact which were available to Sir George Warner for his edition of the Egerton text. None of these MSS give complete names and forms of all alphabets: no two are alike in what they omit, but all omit something. The names of the letters are, as usual, fairly stable and pure. The forms, however, are highly corrupt. Unfortunately, Sir George Warner, to whom we owe the only important study of the problem, had access to these MSS only. He realised that the forms were too corrupt to be useful, and was able only to draw his inferences from the names of the letters. But the problem of the alphabets can only be solved, if at all, by a study of the forms, and for this we have to look for copies less corrupt than any hitherto available. Luckily such copies exist. As we have seen, a comparatively incorrupt exemplar of the 'first family' is preserved in the Paris MS 4515. The 'second family' is found in von Diemeringen's German translation (in the printed edition of 1484 and still better in the MS Add. 17335 in the British Museum) and in MS 10420 of the Bibliothèque Royale, Brussels.

Up to now two works, both heavy with learning, have been called in aid to help with the elucidation of the problem. The first is J. G. Eccard's *De Origine Germanorum, libri duo*, 1750, and the *Cosmographica* of Aethicus (see Pertz, *De Cosmographica Aethici libri tres*, Berlin, 1853). Eccard (pl. XIV, facing p. 188, not pl. IV, p. 192, as Warner says, and after him Hamelius), reproduces alphabets from a Ratisbon MS, said to date from the eleventh century (the whereabouts of which is now unknown), which gives the same names of the letters as Mandeville's Egyptian, Hebrew and Persian. Sir George Warner points out the identity of the names of the letters with Mandeville's, but their forms are even more important. Pertz reproduces Aethicus' alphabet in versions drawn from six MSS, the earliest dating from the eighth century, while the others range from the tenth to the twelfth century.[1]

A third source has now come to light in the *A.b.c. Buch, oder Grundliche Anweisung, in welcher der zarten Jugend . . . in der Teutsch, Lateinisch . . . den meisten Orientalischen Sprachen . . . ein leichter Weg gezeiget wird,* published (and compiled?) by Christian Friedrich Gessner, Leipzig, 1743. This Gessner does not seem to have been related to the great scholar J. M. Gessner. He was a Leipzig printer who died in 1740. His book is an uncritical work, but it contains three alphabets (Gessner, pp. 74, 75) relevant to Mandeville, which are often superior both in names and forms to their rivals. They purport to be Egyptian, Saracen and Syrian. From what work Gessner took these alphabets is not known. He gives neither source nor date, but that they and the Mandeville and Ratisbon alphabets have a common origin seems to be beyond doubt. The odd thing about this odd book, which can have been of little use to the tender youth of any age, is that it forms a kind of link between hieroglyphs so corrupt that, without this 'middle term,' no connection could be proved. As Gessner's alphabets are neither more nor less corrupt than Ratisbon's, it is reasonable to assign to them a similar date, that is, one considerably prior to Mandeville.

It is not, of course, to be supposed that Mandeville actually used any one of these sources. His alphabets in fact agree sometimes with one, sometimes with another, or again offer independent readings preferable to any. He

---

[1] It has not been previously noticed that this alphabet is also quoted, as from Aethicus, along with a correct Hebrew, Greek and Runic, in Hrabanus Maurus, *De Inventione Linguarum* (Migne, CXII, 1579), which is on the whole more likely to have been accessible to Mandeville than Aethicus.

therefore used a source or sources now lost, but belonging to the same family as the others. The importance of Ratisbon, Aethicus and Gessner lies in their proof that Mandeville's alphabets (with the exception of Cathayan and Pentexoire) are not inventions, and in the indications which, in conjunction with Mandeville, they will be found to give of the real sources of these wild and incredible corruptions. It is on them, with the only good copy of Mandeville's 'first family,' (Bib. Nat. Nouv. Acq. 4515) and the three exemplars of his 'second family' (von Diemeringen, 1484, Add. MSS 17335, and Bibl. Roy. Brussels 10420) that any attempt to explain the Mandeville alphabets must be based.

The alphabets, in order of their occurrence, are:

Greek: This presents no problem, for all our four sources are evidently derived in names and forms from genuine Greek, All but one, however, are considerably corrupt, showing that their scribes can have known little, if any, Greek. The exception is the 1484 edition of von Diemeringen, whose Greek is suspiciously correct, while the MS Add. 17335 of von Diemeringen's translation, which is usually superior to the printed version, is markedly corrupt. It may be inferred that someone engaged in its printing knew the Greek alphabet. This is borne out by his spelling 'Beta' phonetically 'Vita,' as it would have been pronounced by a Greek of the period.

Egyptian: This alphabet is found in the Ratisbon MS and in Gessner's 'A.b.c. Buch' as well as in Mandeville. The names do not vary, but bear, so far as can be ascertained, no relation to any known alphabet of any country. The forms vary so extensively in most of our sources that nothing could be safely inferred, except that all must have a common origin. Warner says (p. 172) 'to what language the alphabet here given belongs I cannot tell,' but Brussels 10420 preserves slight but conclusive traces of its source: and this, as might be expected, is Coptic. This language, debased from Ancient Egyptian and equipped with an alphabet based on Greek, has now been extinct for over two centuries, but in Mandeville's time was still holding its own among Egyptian Christians against Arabic. As usual, the foreign alphabet has been forced into correspondence with the Latin order, so that Mandeville's f, g, h are the Coptic zo, zita, ita respectively, while his x, y are really khi and psi.

Hebrew: This is found also in the Ratisbon MS, and Hrabanus Maurus. The names of the letters agree in Ratisbon and Paris 4515, and reproduce with moderate fidelity those of genuine Hebrew. Von Diemeringen gives no names, and his forms are, in fact, those which Paris 4515 later gives as Saracen! Brussels 10420 omits the Hebrew alphabet altogether. The Hebrew forms, therefore, are given by only one of our four Mandeville sources, namely, Paris 4515. They agree reasonably well with Ratisbon, and both will be found to be rather corrupt forms of the genuine Hebrew of the time, as reproduced for example by von Harff in his Travels.[1] It would appear that the scribe of Paris 4515 was as puzzled as later editors have been by the forms he had before him, for he adds a perfect Hebrew alphabet in his appendix, and, to show his mastery of the language, quotes Psalm I, 1 in Hebrew: 'Blessed is the man that walketh not in the counsel of the ungodly.'

Saracen: It is absent in von Diemeringen. In this version the account of Mahometanism and the Saracens, in which the Saracen alphabet normally occurs, is transferred to the end of the book, and it must have been in the course of this transfer that the omission took place. As will be seen, however, von Diemeringen employs the Saracen names of the letters for his Tartar-Russ, and he had already given their forms as Hebrew. Both names and forms of the Saracen alphabet are given in Paris 4515, Brussels 10420 and Gessner. An alphabet with similar names is given in the *Cosmographia* of Aethicus mentioned above. This was

[1] See p. 218, of v. Harff's *Pilgrimage*. Hakluyt Society, 1946.

noticed by Sir George Warner (p. 194) who, having no access to a good exemplar of Mandeville's forms, and therefore forced to judge by names only, was unfortunately led to identify Mandeville's Saracen with the alphabet of Aethicus. But Mandeville's forms are totally unconnected with the alphabet of Aethicus. The names, like those of the Egyptian and Persian, are fanciful, but Mandeville's Saracen forms are in fact Runic, rearranged to follow the order of the Latin alphabet, instead of the Runic (which begins, of course, f, u, th, o, r, c and is hence sometimes known as the Futhorc).[1] An alphabet given by Ratisbon as Arabic is also Runic, and in this case the order is again Latin, but the correct Runic names have been retained for the letters. Why Runic should ever have been mistaken for Arabic, or Saracen, cannot now be known; but since his predecessors fell into the error before him, we can confidently say that it was not Mandeville's fault or invention.

Persian: Versions of both names and forms of this alphabet are to be found in Ratisbon and Gessner, who call it 'Chaldean' and 'Syrian' respectively. Its names appear to be fanciful. The 1484 edition of von Diemeringen presents the forms in a muddled order, which should be checked with the von Diemeringen MS (Add. 17335). The Persian alphabet contains one of many indications that Mandeville's authority was not Ratisbon itself, but a source different from and sometimes superior to Ratisbon. All our four Mandeville examples rightly have a letter 'vith = u' which Ratisbon lacks. For the genuine origin of this Persian, see the remarks below on the Chaldean alphabet.

Chaldean: In form this alphabet is identical with that in the Cosmographia of Aethicus and quoted by Hrabanus Maurus. Its names, however, are evidently an abbreviation of those of Mandeville's Persian; and comparison of its forms with those of Mandeville's Persian and Ratisbon's

---

[1] See I. Taylor *The Alphabet*, ii, 218 for reproduction and discussion of Runic.

Chaldean raises a suspicion that these alphabets are intimately related. This suspicion is strengthened by Gessner's Syrian, which resembles Mandeville's Persian more closely than his Chaldean, but forms a link between the two. Proof comes from Brussels 10420, whose Persian and Chaldean have diverged less extensively than elsewhere, and, indeed, are extremely similar. The Persian and Chaldean alphabets are in fact doublets, and why this is so, and why they should appear under the three names of Persian, Chaldean and Syrian, is explained by I. Taylor in *The Alphabet* (vol. I, p. 292): 'The Christians of Persia were exclusively Nestorian . . . The Nestorian or, as it is sometimes called, the Syro-Chaldaic alphabet, is merely the Syriac alphabet as it was used in the Sassanian realm.' Just as Mandeville gave Coptic as Egyptian, he has again given the alphabet used by the Christians, not the pagan inhabitants of the country. His Persian and Chaldean alphabets are not very similar to the genuine Nestorian alphabet given by Taylor (*The Alphabet*, vol. I, p. 288), but they clearly resemble the rather corrupt version of Nestorian-Syrian taken by von Harff from Breydenbach's *Peregrinationes*.[1] Whether Mandeville's Persian and Chaldean originate from the respective forms of the Nestorian alphabet used in those countries it is impossible, in view of their corruptions, to say, but that they, and therefore the Aethicus alphabet come from *some* version of Nestorian is now evident.

Tartar-Russ : This occurs only in von Diemeringen's translation, being absent even from Brussels 10420. Apart from its occurrence only in a text containing Ogier interpolations (see above, p. 107), this alphabet is highly suspect, for its names are those of the Saracen, omitted by von Diemeringen but present in our other exemplars, and its forms are later given by von Diemeringen as Cathayan. It seems probable that this alphabet is a 'ghost,' manufactured from the Saracen names and Cathayan forms.

[1] See von Harff, p. 150.

Cathayan and Pentexoire: these may conveniently be taken together. They both occur in von Diemeringen and in Brussels 10420, and not elsewhere. The Pentexoire letters are nameless in both, while the Cathayan are nameless in Brussels 10420 and in the 1484 edition of von Diemeringen, but in von Diemeringen's MS (Add. 17335) they bear the same names as Tartar-Russ. The Pentexoire alphabet is reproduced by Cordier in his edition of Friar Odoric (p. 442).[1] Between Cathayan and Pentexoire in von Diemeringen there is little resemblance, even if we follow the purer version of Add. 17335. But if we add the evidence of Brussels 10420, it is seen that all but two or three letters, at least, are closely related. These alphabets, therefore, like Persian and Chaldean, are doublets; but for them, alone among the Mandeville alphabets, it has not been possible to find either a source, or an origin in a genuine alphabet.

It will be noticed that the last three alphabets, Tartar-Russ, Cathayan, and Pentexoire are highly suspicious. Tartar-Russ is a 'ghost,' Cathayan and Pentexoire are doublets, and come from an inaccessible and a fabulous country respectively. All three lack the pedigree originating in a genuine alphabet which the other Mandeville alphabets possess. But they have another characteristic in common: all three are found only in texts which are otherwise remarkable for having Ogier interpolations. It has already been suggested (above p. 107) that the interpolations dealing with the exploits of Ogier the Dane were inserted by Jean d'Outremeuse, who was Mandeville's executor and friend. It is reasonable to suppose that these suspect alphabets came, like the Ogier interpolations, from Jean d'Outremeuse himself, and that they are invented.

[1] He states that it comes from Mandeville, but does not say whether from a printed edition or MS. Hamelius (vol. II p. 184, c. 32, note) wrongly states that Cordier's reproduction is a facsimile from Brussels 10420, from which in reality it diverges widely. It is in fact taken from the edition of von Diemeringen printed at Basel in 1481 by Bernhard Richel, reproductions of whose illustrations and alphabets will be found in A. Schramm, *Der Bilderschmuck, der Frühdrucke*, Bd. 21, and differs only minutely from the same alphabet in the edition of 1484.

To sum up:

Greek: presents no problems.

Egyptian: based on Coptic.

Hebrew: genuine but corrupt, except in Paris 4515.

Saracen: based on Runic.

Persian: ⎫
Chaldean: ⎬ doublets based on Nestorian.

Tartar-Russ: a 'ghost,' manufactured from Saracen and Cathayan.

Cathayan: ⎫ doublets. No source has been discovered,
Pentexoire: ⎬ probably invented. [1]

CHAPTER XVIII

Farewell

THE author of the 'Travels' is now home again at Liége, and we have reached the end of the book. After claiming to have spent thirty-four years travelling about the world, Mandeville sits down and says farewell. His epilogue deserves careful study, for it tells us what kind of man the author was, and is very moving in its simplicity. Indeed, it is difficult to read the epilogue to-day without believing that every word that Mandeville wrote was true. I quote from the Cotton version, which is fuller than the others. It appears only in the English translations.

And ye shall understand, if it like you, that at mine home-coming, I came to Rome, and shewed my life to our holy father, the Pope, and was assoiled of all that lay in my conscience, of many a diverse grievous point; as men must needs that be in company, dwelling amongst so many a diverse folk of diverse sect and of belief, as I have been.

And amongst all I shewed him this treatise, that I had made after information of men that knew of things that I had not seen myself, and also of marvels and customs that I had seen myself, as far as God would give me grace; and besought his holy fatherhood, that my book might be examined and corrected by the advice of his wise and discreet council. And our holy father, of his special grace, remitted my book to be examined and proved by the advice of his said counsel. By the which my book was proved for true, insomuch that they shewed me a book, that my book was examined by, that comprehended full much more, by an hundred part, by the which the *Mappa Mundi*[1] was made after. And so my book (albeit that many men ne list not to give credence to nothing, but to that that they see with their eye, ne be the author ne the person never so true) is

[1] As to the *Mappa Mundi*, see above, p. 101.

L 161

affirmed and proved by our holy father, in manner and form as I have said.

And I, John Mandeville, Knight, aforesaid (although I be unworthy) that departed from our countries and passed the sea, the year of grace a thousand three hundred and twenty two, that passed many lands and many isles and countries, and searched many full strange places, and have been in many a full good honourable company, and at many a fair deed of arms (albeit that I did none myself, for mine unable insuffisance) now I am come home, maugre myself, to rest, for gouts artetykes that me distrain, that define the end of my labour; against my will (God knoweth). And thus taking solace in my wretched rest, recording the time passed, I have fulfilled these things and put them written in this book, as it would come into my mind, the year of grace a thousand three hundred and fifty six, in the thirty-fourth year that I departed from our countries.[1]

The author then begs his readers to pray for him, as he will pray for them, hoping that God will forgive his sins, and make him and his readers joint partners in eternal bliss. The story about the pope is no doubt spurious. It is also a curious blunder, as between 1305 and 1378 the popes were at Avignon. Moreover it is difficult to reconcile this statement with the next, that it was not until 1356, when Mandeville had come home (i.e., to England) and was suffering from gout, that he wrote his book to solace his rest, but these fictions are not of great importance. All that matters is the book.

It would be a thousand pities if the detailed and often complicated problems discussed in these pages should distract attention from the narrative itself. Mandeville's 'Travels' was a new venture in literature. It is true that the book sets out to be a guide to the Holy land, but it soon becomes clear that its main purpose is simply to entertain and amuse. When one realises that the work is a compilation, involving a prodigious memory and much reading, which incidentally can have left little time for wandering about the world, the

---

[1] It is interesting to note that Dr. Johnson selected this passage in his Dictionary 'for the force of thought and beauty of expression.' Todd's edition, 1827, I, p. 43–4.

skill with which the innumerable threads are gathered up, and the whole book presented as a continuous personal narrative, is amazing. The details are ingenious and well devised. The author is never overwhelmed by his authorities. He is never dull. He has no axe to grind, except possibly when his dislike for the papacy gets the better of him, but too much must not be made of this, for the author's piety is never in doubt. He is pleased to note that Prester John was a Christian, although he and his people had not all the Catholic articles of faith. Some part of his admiration for the Great Chan is undoubtedly due to the fact that, although not a Christian, he suffered Christians to dwell in the land, and that when the Great Chan was in progress and met a company of priests chanting *veni creator spiritus*, and carrying a cross and holy water, he stopped his chariot, doffed his hat, knelt before the cross, and received the blessing of the Church. In his description of the Land of Darkness, where a Persian host, intent on slaughtering Christians, was shrouded and lost in utter darkness, Mandeville is careful to point the moral. If men were only more devout to serve God, no enemy could stand against them, and they would find that the age of miracles was not over. It was due to the grace of God that Mandeville and his companions passed safely through the Valley Perilous, and if Christian men would unite together in prayer, and purge their hearts of covetousness and envy, the infidel would be chased out of the Holy Land, and Jerusalem would be recovered 'for the right heirs of Jesu Christ.'

Throughout the whole book the personal interest predominates. Although the author keeps to the background, he discloses himself, when need arises, as an honest God-fearing man, courteous, dignified, and deeply curious — like Pepys, 'with child' for any new thing — a soldier, with a soldier's love of battle and fair deeds of arms, gouty in his old age, but without complaint or ill-temper, and writing, or appearing to write, as an Englishman, with all an

Englishman's love of travel, and with an Englishman's longing to return home at last and die in peace.

How deftly and with what a genius for under-statement the personal touches are introduced ! And when that method fails the gap is supplied by question and answer. The author is represented as a great questioner, asking questions privily and setting down the answers with the skill of a modern newspaper reporter. And the colours are never too high or the shadows too black. Indeed, the language is always a little lower in tone than the marvels described. His disclaimers have the very air of truth. Obviously the reader's credulity must not be strained to breaking point. The Fountain of Youth gave him health, but not immortality. He knew the way to the Earthly Paradise, but had not been there, not being worthy. He had not visited the Land of Darkness, nor had he seen the man-eating giants in an island beyond the Valley Perilous. He had not been to Tartary, which was a country only fit for dogs to live in. Nor had he seen the daughter of Ypocras in the isle of Lango, in form and likeness of a dragon. We have to try and imagine what effect these stories would have on the average reader at that time, and there can be little doubt, I think, that the author's disavowals — 'this I saw not': 'I have not been so far above upward': 'I went never by that way': 'I was not there,' and so on — must have carried as much, if not more, conviction than any number of positive assertions. After all, negative evidence has its value in every age and in every walk of life.

When direct affirmative statements occur they are impressive enough. 'This I saw.' 'I did great business for to have learned that craft.' 'When I was there.' 'Of that fruit I have eaten.' 'And he [the Sultan of Egypt] would have married me full highly to a great Prince's daughter, if I would have forsaken my law and my belief, but I thank God I had no will to do it, for nothing that he behight me' — these assertions are introduced with great skill, just when the reader's attention might begin to flag. And there is one piece of direct evidence which must have convinced the most hardened unbeliever. In the description of the Valley Perilous it is stated that Mandeville and his companions were attacked by devils, who not only frightened the travellers badly, but inflicted upon them many grievous and dolorous blows. As a result, Mandeville is made to say that he carried home with him on his body a black mark the size of a hand, which persisted for eighteen years until he fell to his prayers, when it vanished miraculously, leaving the skin whiter than before. This mark was certainly not come by in the Valley Perilous, for the author was never there, but it must have been exhibited to many worthy people in Liége during those eighteen years, and even when it had disappeared, the white scar remained to recall the incident, and warn would-be travellers against similar escapades.

If we wished to be harsh with Mandeville it would be easy to dismiss him as a liar, with leanings towards superstition and the black arts, but he was largely, if not wholly, a child of his age, and posterity must take him as it finds him. And at least we must give him credit for broad mindedness. Writing of the Brahmans, he is careful to point out that they were people of good faith and holy lives, and that God must love them, just as he loved Job, who was a paynim. 'And therefore, albeit that there be many diverse laws in the world, yet I trow that God loveth always them that love him, and serve him meekly in truth, and namely them that despise the vain glory of this world, as this folk do, and as Job did also.' Here speaks a true Christian with a freedom of outlook far in advance of his time. His book, which is not too long, but just long enough, must have given pleasure to countless readers in all ages and countries, and that is fame enough. For himself, Mandeville made no claim upon posterity. He wrote for his contemporaries and was content to leave the book to take care of itself. 'He that will trow it, trow it, and he that will not, leave.'

Bibliography (I)

(a) LATIN VERSIONS

The Latin versions fall into two groups, the version known as the vulgate (which has been printed), and four independent versions, not printed. See Vogels *Die ungedruckten Lateinischen Versionen Mandeville's*, Crefeld, 1886, and Röhricht, *Bibliotheca Geog. Palaestinae*, Berlin, 1890, pp. 79–85. The vulgate text is notable as the earliest text containing references to the exploits of Ogier the Dane (above, p. 107). The other Latin versions contain no Ogier passages. The Latin MSS have no illustrations and no alphabets. It is an odd circumstance that, with one exception, the MSS of the four independent Latin versions are all in English libraries, and that the exception (No. 5) was written by an Englishman, a monk at Abingdon Abbey.

VULGATE TEXT

1. BRITISH MUSEUM, Harley 3589: fifteenth century.
2. BRITISH MUSEUM, Add. 37, 512: dated 1457.
3. OXFORD, BODLEIAN, Laud 721: fifteenth century.
4. OXFORD, BODLEIAN, Fairfax 23: c. 1450.

INDEPENDENT LATIN VERSIONS

5. LEYDEN UNIVERSITY LIBRARY, Vulcanii No. 96: dated 1390. The copyist adds the date and his name Richard Bledeclewe, a monk of Abingdon Abbey. No illustrations except an illuminated border and on p. 91 a circle with the signs of the Zodiac nicely drawn in red and purple, illustrating ch. XXIII. No alphabets. See Vogels, op. cit. p. 5, and *Codices Manuscripti Bibliothecae Universitatis Leidenensis* (Lugd. Bat. 1910), I, p. 39.
6. BRITISH MUSEUM, Egerton 672: late fourteenth or early fifteenth cent. The text agrees in the main with 5, but is incomplete. It stops

short in the middle of the chapter on the roundness of the earth (Pollard, ch. xx). No illustrations, no alphabets, no Ogier stories.

7. BRITISH MUSEUM, Harley 82: fifteenth cent. Imperfect at beginning and end. A different version from 5 and 6. No illustrations, no alphabets, no Ogier passages.

8. BRITISH MUSEUM, Royal 13 E. IX: c. 1400. This is a third independent version, possibly the version from which the shortened French translations printed by Warner were made. No illustrations, no alphabets, no Ogier stories. Vogels suggests that this was the Latin text which the translator of the Egerton version had by him. Vogels, op. cit. p. 21. Miscalled by Vogels Harley 13 E. IX.

9. BRITISH MUSEUM, Cotton App. 59: fifteenth cent. similar to, if not identical with, 8.

10. BRITISH MUSEUM, Harley 175: fifteenth cent. Similar to, if not identical with, 8 and 9.

11. GLASGOW, HUNTERIAN MUSEUM. T. 4. I: fifteenth cent. Bound up with versions of Odoric of Pordenone and Marco Polo. Apparently similar to, if not identical with, 8, 9 and 10. See *Catalogue* by Young and Aitkin, Glasgow, 1908, No. 84.

12. OXFORD, BODLEIAN, Ashmole 769: c. 1450. A fourth independent version.
Apart from the vulgate text we have therefore four different Latin versions: (1) Vulcanii 96 and Egerton 672; (2) Harley 82; (3) Royal 13 E. IX, Cotton App. 59, Harley 175, Hunterian Museum T. 4. I, (4) Ashmole 769.

13. GEORGE A. PLIMPTON LIBRARY, NEW YORK CITY, No. 264. Written at Liége, 1456. De Ricci and Wilson, *Census of Medieval and Renaissance MSS in U.S.A.*, p. 1801. This may possibly belong to the vulgate class.

For other Latin texts in Berlin, Gotha, Dresden, Vienna, Trier, Liége, Brussels, Copenhagen, Turin, see Vogels, op. cit., p. 6–7; Röhricht, op. cit., and generally Beazley, *Dawn of Modern Geography*, III, p. 549.

(b) ENGLISH VERSIONS

It is possible to arrive at some grouping of the English versions (references: C = Cotton, E = Egerton, D = Defective Text, i.e., the text printed before 1725).

C and E are in a group by themselves. So are E. Museo 116 and Rawl. D. 99. All others have the gap in the description of Egypt, and all, except E. Museo 116 and Rawl. D. 99, have the story that the book was submitted to the Pope at Rome. It follows that all known English MSS, with the above exceptions, belong to D, and have a common origin, although there are minor variations. There is other confirmation. If we take the four complete versions of D at the British Museum (see Nos. 16, 17, 18 and 21) we find that they have the same tally of alphabets — Hebrew and Saracen only, both names and forms. This is true of the Castle Howard MS (No. 32).

As to the English versions generally there are two schools of thought:

Warner and Nicholson; D is the earliest. C and E are expansions of D by writers who had recourse to a French original.

Vogels; E is based on D. D, C and E are at base one translation. D derives from C because there is good evidence that C is a direct translation from the French and, if it be granted that a single translation from the French is the base of C and D, then D derives from C. E. Museo 116 and Rawl. D.99 contain English versions made from the Latin.

The best statement of this difficult problem known to me is by Mr. Kenneth Sisam in *Fourteenth Century Verse and Prose*, Oxford, 1921, p. 240., but, as he points out, an investigator who wished to clear the ground would have to face the labour of preparing a six-text Mandeville based on French, C, D, E, Latin, and the English versions, in E. Museo 116 and Rawl. D, 99, a task not to be lightly undertaken.

---

14. BRITISH MUSEUM, Cotton Titus C. XVI: 1410–20. The Cotton text, lacking 3 ff. after fo. 53. So far as is known it is the only MS of the Cotton text in existence. For a description see p. 127, and generally p. 122. No illustrations. *Alphabets*: Greek, Egyptian, Hebrew, Saracen, both names and forms.

15. BRITISH MUSEUM, Egerton 1982: 1410–20. The Egerton text. See above p. 133 for a description. So far as is known this is the

only MS of this version in existence. It has been printed. See under Warner. No illustrations. *Alphabets*: Greek names and forms, Egyptian names, Hebrew names and forms, Saracen in two versions, both names and forms, Persian names and Chaldean forms only. The letters are boldly and carefully drawn. The MS was first noticed by E. W. B. Nicholson. See Letter to 'THE ACADEMY' 11 Nov. 1876.

16. BRITISH MUSEUM, Harley 3954: early fifteenth cent. This is apparently the ancestor or near relative of the Defective Text. Copious illustrations in ink coloured with red, green and blue. Some are unfinished and blank spaces left for others. The illustrations are at times crude, but often spirited and amusing. *Alphabets*: Hebrew and Saracen names and forms — carefully drawn in red ink.

17. BRITISH MUSEUM, Arundel 140: fifteenth cent. Copied possibly from 16. No illustrations. *Alphabets*: Hebrew and Saracen names and forms. A finely-written MS.

18. BRITISH MUSEUM, Royal 17 C. XXXVIII: early fifteenth cent. An abridged version (see 16). Numerous illustrations with free use of gold-leaf and blue and red; archaic in style, but some quaint and amusing. *Alphabets*: Hebrew and Saracen names and forms.

19. BRITISH MUSEUM, Add. 37049: first half of fifteenth cent. Only 13 pp. of an abridged version. There is a map showing three continents divided by a T-shaped ocean, and a picture of Jerusalem with some twenty buildings within a wall. No other illustrations, no alphabets.

20. BRITISH MUSEUM, Sloane 2319: early fifteenth cent. Incomplete at beginning and end. There are other defects. No illustrations. *Alphabets*: Saracen names and forms.

21. BRITISH MUSEUM, Royal 17 B. XLIII: fifteenth cent. An abridged version. No illustrations. *Alphabets*: Hebrew and Saracen names and forms. A beautifully-written MS with some amusing marginal notes:—'a goude tale': 'a tale of fayry': 'all men gon there naked' and so on. (See illustration, p. 145).

22. BRITISH MUSEUM, Add. 33758: fifteenth cent. A poor text. A note by Mr. Douce, undated, reads as follows: 'Mr. Rodd. I return your MS Mandeville, because it agrees word for word with one that I have, and as it came from the author's family (!) this agreement may add to the value of yours.' The Douce MS referred to is now Douce 109 in the Bodleian. No illustrations, no alphabets.

23. BRITISH MUSEUM, Harley 2386: fifteenth cent. An abridged text. No illustrations. *Alphabets*: Hebrew names and forms.

24. BRITISH MUSEUM, Add. 24189. No text, but a collection of twenty-eight beautiful fifteenth-century miniatures illustrating the earlier part of Mandeville, reproduced in Warner's edition of the Egerton text for the Roxburghe Club. The last passage illustrated is ch. v. It is unfortunate that the artist should have stopped there, for there are no pictures of the Far East.

25. OXFORD, BODLEIAN, E. Museo 116: 1420–50. A much abbreviated text; one of the four English versions without the gap in the description of Egypt, and one of the two English versions without the story that the book was submitted to the Pope at Rome. The copyist or translator has taken considerable liberties with the text. Some episodes are omitted, others are re-arranged. Prologue and Epilogue, which differ from other English versions, are given by Vogels, *Englische Version*, p. 15. If it ever becomes possible to publish a collection of English versions this and the next MS would be entitled to a place of honour. The language is vigorous, even racy, and most of the best stories are included. Vogels (p. 46) thinks that this and the next version are translations from the Latin, Royal 13, E. IX (above No. 8) with assistance from the Leyden MS (No. 5), and that this MS was the version from which the Egerton translator filled in the gaps in the Defective Text. No illustrations or alphabets.

26. OXFORD, BODLEIAN. Rawlinson D 99: fifteenth cent. As with E. Museo 116 the text is much abbreviated. No Egypt gap. No story about the Pope. No illustrations or alphabets.

Other English MSS in the Bodleian, not calling for special notice, are Addit. C. 285; Laud 699, Rawlinson B.216 and D.101, Douce 109 and 33; Rawlinson D.100, E. Museo 124, Tanner 405, Ashmole 751. All are described by Vogels, op. cit. pp. 14–17. Douce 109 contains the following note in an eighteenth century hand. 'N.B. I had this Book from a Descendant by the Mother's side from Sir John Mandeville. W.T.' We could wish for more information ! See above No. 22. Vogels also describes MSS in Queen's Coll. No. 383 and Balliol Coll. 239.

27. HENRY E. HUNTINGTON LIBRARY, SAN MARINO, H.M.114; fifteenth cent., containing also texts of 'Piers Plowman' and

Chaucer's 'Troilus and Criseyde.' De Ricci and Wilson, *Census of Medieval and Renaissance MSS in U.S.A.*, p. 51.

28. CAMBRIDGE UNIVERSITY LIBRARY, Dd. 1. 17: fifteenth cent. A finely-written MS which begins in vol. III. No illustrations. *Alphabets*: Saracen and Hebrew names and forms. There are illuminated letters and some amusing marginal notes — 'A gode tale,' 'A tale of fayre,' 'All men go naked,' 'none hedes,' 'on eye,' and so on.

29. CAMBRIDGE, UNIVERSITY LIBRARY, Gg. I. 34.3: fifteenth cent. A badly-written MS with letters picked out in red. No illustrations. *Alphabet*: Saracen names and forms.

30. CAMBRIDGE, UNIVERSITY LIBRARY, Ff.5.35: fifteenth cent. A finely-written MS, but incomplete. No illustrations. *Alphabets*: Saracen and Hebrew names and forms.

Vogels mentions also the following MSS at Cambridge: fifteenth century, Trinity Coll: R 4.20; Pepysian Library (Magdalene Coll:) No. 1955.

31. MR. BOIES PENROSE of Philadelphia: fifteenth cent. A well-written MS with illuminated initial and border on fo. 1^R and a drawing of a woman on fo. 22^R. No other illustrations. *Alphabets*: Saracen and Hebrew names and forms. The Egypt gap occurs on f.19, and the story about the Pope on f. 42. Owned formerly by the Giffard family of Chillington Park, Staffs.

32. CASTLE HOWARD LIBRARY: fifteenth cent., now (1948) in the possession of Mr. Lionel Robinson, the well-known bookseller of Pall Mall, who has kindly allowed me to study it. It was known to Vogels (*Englische Version*, p. 17) but not seen by him. It is described in Bernard's *Cat. librorum Manuscriptorum Angliae et Hiberniae*, Oxford, 1674, II, p. 14. No. 613, as 'The History of Sir John Mandevil compleat in Old English'. Unfortunately the MS is not 'compleat.' It lacks several leaves of the Prologue. It belongs to the Defective class. There are no illustrations. *Alphabets*: Hebrew and Saracen, both names and forms. The Egypt gap occurs at f. 13 and the story about the Pope at f. 99.

33. CHETHAM'S LIBRARY, MANCHESTER. fifteenth cent. Double columns, much rubricated. No illustrations. *Alphabet*: Saracen only. The Egypt gap occurs on f. 14, and the story about the Pope on f. 78.

(c) FRENCH VERSIONS

The earliest French MS is in the Bibliothèque Nationale, Paris. It has not been printed and it is of great interest, both for its contents and its history. I have been supplied with photostats.

34. PARIS, BIBLIOTHÈQUE NATIONALE, Nouv. Acq. Franç. 4515. The MS is written in a minuscule bookhand of fine quality. It was written by Rauolet d'Orleans for Maître Gervaise Crestien, first physician to Charles V of France, a notable collector of books. It is dated 18 Sept. 1371. It is followed by a treatise on the plague (written by the same scribe) by John de Bourgogne, *dit à la barbe*, professor of medicine in Liége (see above p. 18). According to the colophon this treatise was compiled in 1365. The Mandeville MS contains the following illustrations. On the frontispiece is a painting in four compartments, showing Mandeville writing, in audience with some eastern potentate, either the Sultan or the Great Chan or Prester John, and two scenes showing the story of the daughter of Hypocras (see above, p. 43). On fo. 34 there is a picture of the Transfiguration, and on fo. 37 a picture of St. Paul with a drawn sword, and St. Luke with a winged ox or calf hovering over his head. There are six finely drawn alphabets, Greek, Egyptian, Hebrew, Saracen, Persian and Chaldean. The Greek, Egyptian and Chaldean are omitted from the text and placed together at the end. There is a pseudo-Hebrew alphabet in the text, and a perfectly genuine one at the end (fo. 97).

According to an entry in Giles Malet's catalogue of the Louvre Library (1373), the volume was withdrawn by Charles V on 20 November 1392. It was returned intact in the seventeenth cent. and remained there until it was stolen in 1841 or 1842, when the works were separated. Both treatises passed into the possession of the Earl of Ashburnham, but were returned to Paris in the nineteenth century. The two works are now bound together again. The book was probably stolen by Joseph Barrois (b. 1785, d. 1855), a member of the Chamber of Deputies, who, with Count Libri-Carrucci, was involved in a number of thefts and other frauds. An account of their activities is given in 'Notes and Queries,' 192, p. 495 (15.11.47).

The MS is of importance for three reasons:—(1) It is the earliest known MS of Mandeville's 'Travels,' (2) It associates

Mandeville with de Bourgogne, (3) It contains the passage quoted above (p. 21) which shows that the book was written originally in French, and not in Latin, as stated in the Cotton version.

The following four MSS, mentioned by Vogels (*Italienische Version*, pp. 40, 42) are similar to Paris 4515; and see Beazley, *Dawn of Modern Geography*, III, p. 549.

35. BIBLIOTHÈQUE NATIONALE, PARIS, Arsenal 3219 (c. 1400).

36. BIBLIOTHÈQUE NATIONALE, PARIS, MS franç. 24436 (dated 1396).

37. BIBLIOTHÈQUE NATIONALE, PARIS, MS franç. 5637 (c.1400).

38. BIBLIOTHÈQUE NATIONALE, PARIS, MS franç. 6109 (fifteenth century).

39. BRITISH MUSEUM, Harley 4383: late fourteenth cent., written in England. This text, supplemented by the next three MSS, was printed by Warner (H) in his edition of the Egerton version. There are no illustrations. *Alphabets*: Greek, Egyptian, Hebrew, both names and forms. The MS is incomplete, ending in the middle of ch. XXII.

40. BRITISH MUSEUM, Royal 20 B.X: fifteenth cent. Written in England. Warner's R. No illustrations. *Alphabets*: Greek, Egyptian and Hebrew names only.

41. BRITISH MUSEUM, Sloane 1464: late fourteenth cent. Written in England. Warner's S. No illustrations. *Alphabets*: Egyptian and Hebrew names and forms. Greek forms are given as Saracen.

42. BRITISH MUSEUM, Add. 33,757, formerly Grenville XXXIX: late fourteenth cent. Warner's G. No illustrations. *Alphabets*: Greek names only. Egyptian, Hebrew, Saracen, Persian and Chaldean names and forms. This MS is the most complete French MS (apart from No. 34) so far as alphabets are concerned.

43. BRITISH MUSEUM, Harley 212: no date. Warner's family. No illustrations. *Alphabets*: Greek, Egyptian, Hebrew and Saracen names and forms.

44. BRITISH MUSEUM, Harley 3940: fifteenth cent. apparently not belonging to Warner's family. No illustrations. *Alphabets*: Greek names, Egyptian names and forms. A poor copy. The proper names are disfigured and often unrecognisable.

45. BRITISH MUSEUM, Sloane 560: fifteenth cent. A poor MS of the same family as Warner's. No illustrations, no alphabets.

46. BRITISH MUSEUM, Harley 204, no date. A poor MS of Warner's family. No illustrations. *Alphabets*: Greek and Egyptian names and forms.

47. BRITISH MUSEUM, Harley 1739: no date. Warner's family. No illustrations. *Alphabets*: Greek, Egyptian and Hebrew, names and forms.

48. BRITISH MUSEUM, Royal 20. A.I. fifteenth century. Warner's family. No illustrations, no alphabets.

49. BRUSSELS, BIBLIOTHÈQUE ROYALE, 10420: late fifteenth or early sixteenth cent. See above page 115. Important as the only known French text to contain Ogier stories. *Alphabets*: Greek, Egyptian, Saracen, Chaldean, Cathayan and Pentexoire. I have been supplied with microfilms.

50. HARVARD COLLEGE LIBRARY, Riant, 50: fifteenth cent. Ricci and Wilson, *Census*, p. 1005.

(d) ITALIAN VERSIONS

No Italian MSS of the fourteenth century have been found. Vogels, *Italienische Version*, shows that the Italian versions of the 'Travels' are translated from the French, and he draws attention to some amusing errors in translation.

51. ASHBURNHAM LIBRARY, Libri 1699: fifteenth cent. An important MS, the earliest known, described by Vogels, p. 39. The name Libri suggests that this MS was one of those stolen by Libri and sold to Lord Ashburnham (see No. 34). Many of these MSS were subsequently returned to Paris and I had hoped to find this important MS in the Bibl. Nationale, but it is not there and I have been unable to trace it. From what Vogels says, it would appear to differ little from the printed version (No. 19).

52. PIERPOINT MORGAN LIBRARY, No. 746: 1465, written in Ferrara. De Ricci and Wilson, *Census*, p. 1495.

(e) GERMAN VERSIONS

Röhricht, *op. cit.* p. 81 has a long list of German MSS, mostly in Germany, many of which must be now inaccessible.

53. BRITISH MUSEUM, Add. 18026: 1449. A different translation from both Von Diemeringen and Velser. Written by Johann Segnitz de Castel in 1449. No illustrations, no alphabets.

54. BRITISH MUSEUM, Add 10129: fifteenth cent. Same translation as Add. 18026.

55. BRITISH MUSEUM, Add. 17335: fifteenth cent. A MS version of von Diemeringen's translation, but illustrations by a different artist, probably Dutch, and poor of their kind. All alphabets are given as in von Diemeringen's printed edition and rather less corruptly, and are neatly drawn with alternate letters in red and blue. Some leaves are missing.

56. NEW YORK PUBLIC LIBRARY (Velser's translation). In 1938 this MS was in the possession of the bookseller A. Rosenthal, then of 14 Curzon Street, W.1. It is dated 1459, with eighty-one coloured drawings. The MS is described as written in a German Gothic cursive hand. The text is said to be the same as Sorg's edition of 1481, but the illustrations differ and some do not appear in the printed edition at all. Rosenthal *Catalogue I, Secular Thought*, No. 25.

(f) IRISH VERSIONS

57. BRITISH MUSEUM, Egerton 1781: fifteenth cent. Made by Fineen MacMahon in 1475. No illustrations, no alphabets.

58. BRITISH MUSEUM. Add. 33993: fifteenth cent. Only two leaves of Mandeville. Said in the Catalogue to represent the opening chapter. For printed version see 'List of Books' under Stokes.

(g) DUTCH VERSIONS

59. LEYDEN, UNIVERSITY LIBRARY, HS.BPL14(f): fifteenth cent.

60. GÖTTINGEN, UNIVERSITY LIBRARY, Histor. 828 b: fifteenth cent.

61. BRUSSELS, BIBLIOTHÈQUE ROYALE, 720: fifteenth cent.

62. THE HAGUE, ROYAL LIBRARY, Y. 302 (1191): dated 1462.

All described in N. A. Cramer's Dutch edition of the 'Travels.' See 'List of Books' under Cramer.

63. CAPE TOWN, SOUTH AFRICAN PUBLIC LIBRARY: 15th cent. Written in a Gothic book-hand of fine quality, with an illuminated capital letter, and on fo. 2 a striking picture showing a circular globe supported by four angels, with Mandeville sailing in a boat across a blue sea, with his book open before him. Several islands are shown, with churches and castles. There is a picture of a camel and another animal. Four winds are shown

blowing through trumpets. The globe is surrounded by clouds and stars. The clouds are blue, the stars gold. The angels are clad in flowing draperies of blue and brown. *Alphabets*: Greek, Hebrew, Saracen, Persian and Chaldean names and forms. Egyptian forms only. See *Tijdschrift voor nederlandsche taal – en Letterkunde*, Pt. 30 (1910) pp. 1–53, (article by A. Lodewyckx). This MS was formerly in the possession of Sir George Gray, the Governor of Cape Colony. I have been supplied with photostats. See my note in *Quarterly Bulletin of the S.A. Library*, June, 1949 (Cape Town).

Bibliography (II)

PRINTED EDITIONS, MAINLY BEFORE 1600

This list is intended to be representative rather than complete. For further details of printed editions, see Hain-Copinger; H. Cordier, *Mélanges*, Paris, 1914, I, pp. 1–54; M. B. Stillwell, *Incunabula in American Libraries*, 1940, and the British Museum *Catalogue of XVth century books*. The British Museum references for fifteenth century editions are to this work so far as it has been completed, that is for editions printed in Germany, Italy and France. See also Röhricht, *Bibl. Geog. Palaestinae*, Berlin, 1890, pp. 79–85. STC = *Short Title Catalogue* (Bibliographical Society).

LATIN

The earlier Latin editions are in some cases undated.

1. ZWOLLE, 1483, Pieter van Os. Stillwell, M.137 (Pierpoint Morgan Library). Hain-Copinger, 10645.
2. [STRASSBURG, 1484, Printer of the 1483 'Vitas Patrum']. Stillwell M. 139 (Pierpoint Morgan Library). B.M. C.I. 100 (G.6700). Hain-Copinger, 10643. A fine copy, formerly in the Castle Howard Library, is in my possession.
3. [GOUDA], c. 1485, G. Leeu (not Antwerp, as in B.M. *General Catalogue*). The vulgate text with Odoric interpolations (see above, p. 35). Reprinted by Hakluyt in the 1st ed. of his 'Voyages' (reprint, 1809, vol. II). Chapter headings and numeration. No woodcuts. B.M. IA, 47355. Another copy at G. 6728. A copy, with the Inglis bookplate, from the Sir J. A. Brooke sale, was sold at Sotheby's and bought by Wm. H. Robinson Ltd. on 15 March, 1948, lot 4074. It was bound up with four other works including Marco Polo, Ludolphus de Suchen and Johannes de Hese.
4. [COLOGNE, c. 1500. Cornelis de Zierikzee]. Not Mainz as in B.M. *General Catalogue*. B.M. I.309 (IA, 5204). The vulgate text

without the Odoric interpolations. Minor variations of single words show that it was not printed from the Strassburg 1484 text. No woodcuts, chapter headings or numeration. Stillwell, M.140 (Pierpoint Morgan Library). A copy formerly in the possession of Sir Thomas Brooke was sold at Sotheby's to Quaritch on 15 March, 1948, lot 4073 (Leicester Harmsworth sale, 3rd section). Another is in the library of Mr. Boies Penrose, Philadelphia.

ENGLISH

DEFECTIVE TEXT

5. LONDON [1496?], Richard Pynson. Unique copy in British Museum. G 6713. No woodcuts, no chapter headings. *Alphabets*: Hebrew names, but the forms are merely printed from Pynson's English capitals. Saracen names only. Duff, *English Fifteenth Century Books*, No. 285. STC, 17246. Copinger, 3842.

6. LONDON. 1499, Wynkyn de Worde. Copies in Cambridge University Library and at Stonyhurst (both incomplete). Woodcuts and chapter headings. *Alphabets*: Saracen and Hebrew names and forms. Duff, 286. STC, 17247. Copinger, 3841.

7. LONDON, 1568. Thomas East. Woodcuts and chapter headings. *Alphabets*: Hebrew names and forms. Saracen names only. There are variations from both Pynson and W. de Worde, but there can be little doubt, I think, that East's text is based on W. de Worde. One chapter seems to have dropped out, but many of the woodcuts are identical. One, showing two hermaphrodites in ch. XII, was too crude and realistic for East's public, and had to be toned down. East's edition was the foundation of all reprints down to 1725, and was reprinted in 1932 by the Oxford University Press in a limited edition, the Egypt gap having been filled in from the Cotton version. For other editions before 1640 see STC. Ashton reprinted the Defective Text in 1887 without noticing the Egypt gap.

COTTON TEXT

8. LONDON, 1725, 1727. Reprinted, in 1839, with introduction, notes and glossary, by J. O. Halliwell.
   LONDON, 1900. Modernised by A. W. Pollard.

9. LONDON, 1919–23. Edited by P. Hamelius.

EGERTON TEXT

10. LONDON, 1889. Edited by G. F. Warner.

CHAP-BOOKS

11. LONDON, C. 1720. The Travels and Voyages of Sir John Mandeville, Knt. . . . faithfully collected from the Original Manuscripts, and illustrated with a variety of pictures. Printed for J. Osborne, near Dock-head, Southwark, and James Hodges at the Looking Glass on London Bridge. Price bound, one shilling. This is an honest, although an abridged, edition, based on East, not hack-work like the others. B.M. 10055.a. (I have a copy dated 1704).

12. LONDON, C. 1730. A reprint of the above. B.M. 435a.I.

13. LONDON, C. 1750. Printed and sold in Aldermary Churchyard. Mandeville sets out in 1372. B.M.1079.i.14(23).

14. LONDON, C. 1780. A reprint of the above. B.M.12315.aaa. 6 (3).

15. LONDON, C. 1785. Printed and sold in Bow Church Yard. Less abbreviated than the others. Mandeville sets out in 1732! Some amusing woodcuts. See above p. 125 B.M.1076.l.3 (12). Reprinted by J. Ashton in *Chap Books of the Eighteenth Century*, 1882, p. 405.

FRENCH

16. [LYONS] 1480, Guillaume de Roy. No woodcuts, no chapter headings. A different version from Warner's. B.M. VIII, 235 (G.6775).

17. LYONS [1490], Printer unidentified. Stillwell, M. 141 (Pierpoint Morgan Library). Copinger, 3827.

18. PARIS [c. 1560]. Same version as G.6775.

Cordier, *Mélanges*, p. 21, records other French editions: Lyons, c. 1480; Lyons, 1481; Lyons, c. 1485; Lyons, 1487; Paris, 1550, but I have not been able to trace them.

ITALIAN

19. MILAN, 1480, Petrus de Corneno. No woodcuts or chapter headings. No alphabets. B.M. VI. 758 (G.6702). A copy is in my possession.

20. COLOGNA, 1488, Ugo Rugerius, Same as preceding, as are the following editions. Stillwell. M. 147 (Lessing J. Rosenwald Library). B.M. VI. 808 (G. 6703.

21. BOLOGNA, 1488, Joannes Iacobus: Joannes Antonius de Benedictis. B. M. VI. 835 (G.6706). Stillwell, M. 151 (New York Public Library).

22. VENICE, 1491, Nicolaus de Ferrariis. B.M. V.507 (G.6704). Stillwell, M. 148 (New York Public Library: Harvard College Library).

23. FLORENCE, 1492, Lorenzo Morgiani and G. da Maganza. Mandeville is described on the title-page as 'cavaliere asperondoro [aux éperons d'or] Frazese.' B.M. VI.681 (G.6705;. Stillwell, M. 149 (Library of Congress).

24. VENICE, 1496, Manfredus de Bonellis. B.M. V.504 (G. 6708). Stillwell, M. 150 (University of North Carolina).

25. MILAN, 1497, Uldericus Scinzenzeler. Stillwell M.152 (Henry E. Huntington Library). B.M. VI.772 (IA. 26788).

26. VENICE, 1500, Manfredus de Bonellis and Georgius de Rusconibus. Stillwell, M. 153 (Henry E. Huntington Library).

Ten other editions at the British Museum (the last dated 1567) attest the popularity of Mandeville in Italy. All Italian versions seem to be based on a common original.

SPANISH

27. VALENCIA, 1521, Jorge Costilla. Woodcuts and chapter headings. B.M. c.20. e.32.

28. VALENCIA, 1540. Same as preceding, but woodcuts slightly varied. B.M. c.55. g.4.

29. ALCALA DE HENARES, 1547. Same as preceding. B.M. 149. e.6. As with East and W. de Worde (6 and 7), the woodcut of the hermaphrodites in 27 was too crude for a later public and had to be modified.

GERMAN

VON DIEMERINGEN'S TRANSLATION

30. [BASEL, 1481, Bernard Richel]. Stillwell, M.143 (Library of Congress). Copinger, 3833. There is a full description in W. H. Davies, *Catalogue of German Books in the library of Charles Fairfax Murray*, No. 282. All the woodcuts are reproduced in Schramm, *Der Bilderschmuck der Frühdrucke*, vol. XXI, pl. 398–552.

31. STRASSBURG, 1483, Johann Prüss. Woodcuts, chapter headings, numeration. *Alphabets*: Greek, Egyptian, Hebrew, Tartar-Russ, Persian, Chaldean, Cathayan, Pentexoire. A copy was bought by the New York Public Library at the Landau-Finaly sale at Sotheby's, 13.7.48, lot 79 (microfilms kindly supplied by

the Library). Practically identical with the 1484 edition, but from a different fount. The woodcuts are the same with one exception. In Bk. I, ch IV, an illustration shows Lot in bed with one of his daughters. The 1484 edition omits this, and shows the birth of anti-Christ by means of a Caesarian operation, a most realistic picture. Stillwell, M. 144 (Henry E. Huntington Library). Not in Hain.

32. STRASSBURG, 1484, Johann Prüss. B.M. I.119 (G.6773). The woodcuts in the British Museum copy are coloured by hand. Stillwell, M. 145 (Library of Congress). See above, p. 135. A copy was offered for sale in 1949 by Martin Breslauer, Cat. 67, No. 65.

33. FRANKFURT, 1507. J. Knoblauch. Closely allied to the 1484 edition. B.M. 148. c.8.

34. FRANKFURT, 1580. New and rather indifferent woodcuts.

35. FRANKFURT, 1584. In Feyerabend's 'Reisebuch.' No woodcuts. Text modernised.

VELSER'S TRANSLATION

36. AUGSBURG, 1481, Anton Sorg. Stillwell, M.142 (Pierpoint Morgan Library). Hain, 10647.

37. AUGSBURG, 1482, Von Hannsen Schonsperger. Woodcuts and chapter headings. No alphabets. See above p. 143. B.M. II, 364 (G.6774).

DUTCH

38. ——— c. 1470. Printer and place unidentified. No woodcuts. *Alphabets*: Greek, Egyptian and Saracen names, Chaldean key-letters only. B.M. IB, 48901. Attributed to G. Leeu, Gouda, 1475, by H. Bradshaw, *Collected Papers*, p. 278. Type unique.

CZECH

Röhricht notes the following editions.

PILSEN, 1510, 1513.

PRAGUE, 1576, 1610.

List of Books Consulted

AETHICUS. In Pertz, *De Cosmographica Aethici libri tres*, Berlin, 1853.

ALBERT of AIX. *Alb. Aquensis Hist. Hierosol.* in *Recueil des Historiens des Croisades*, vol. IV., 1879.

ALEXANDER the Great. Most of the Alexander legends are contained in *The Alexander Book in Ethiopia*, by E. A. Wallis Budge, 1933. Every known version is based on the Greek history falsely attributed to Callisthenes, Alexander's companion and friend. The Greek text is printed by Müller, *Pseudo-Callisthenes*, Paris, 1877. The Latin version by Julius Valerius is printed by Müller at the foot of the Greek text. See also Zacher, *Julii Valerii Epitome*, Halle, 1867.

ANDERSON, A. R. *Alexander's Gate, Gog and Magog, and the inclosed Nations*. Monographs of The Medieval Academy of America. No. 5. Cambridge, Massachusetts, 1932 (contains a full Alexander bibliography).

ARCULF. *De Locis Sanctis*, in Tobler, *Itinera et Descriptiones Terrae Sanctae*, Geneva, 1877. Translated by J. R. Macpherson for the Palestine Pilgrims' Text Society, 1889.

ASHTON, JOHN. *The Voiage and Travayle of Sir John Mandeville, Knight*, 1887 (East's text).

——. *Chap. Books of the Eighteenth Century*, 1882.

BALE, JOHN. *Catalogue of British Writers*, in Bishop Tanner's, *Bibliotheca Britannico-Hibernica*, 1748.

BARING-GOULD, S. *Legends of Old Testament Characters*, 1871.

BEAZLEY, C. R. *The Dawn of Modern Geography*, 3 vols. 1897, 1906.

BEVAN, W. L. and PHILLOTT, H. W. *Mediaeval Geography in illustration of the Hereford Mappa Mundi*, 1873.

BOLDENSELE, W. VON. *Itinerarius Guilielmi de Boldensele*, ed. by Grotefend in *Zeitschrift d. histor. Vereins für Niedersachsen*, 1852, pp. 236–86.

BOVENSCHEN, A. 'Untersuchungen über Johann von Mandeville und die Quellen seiner Reisebeschreibung,' in *Zeitschrift der Gesellschaft für Erdkunde zu Berlin*, vol. XXIII, 1888.

BREYDENBACH, B. VON. *Peregrinationes in Terram Sanctam*, 1486 (German translation 1486 and 1488). See under Davies, H. W.

BROWNE, SIR THOMAS. *Enquiries into Vulgar and Common Errors*, in *Works*, ed. by S. Wilkin, 1835, vols. II and III.

BRUNETTO LATINI. *Li Livres deu Tresor* . . .publié pour la premiere fois . . . par P. Chabaille, Paris, 1863.

BULLEIN, WILLIAM. *A Dialogue against the Fever Pestilence*, 1578. Reprinted by Early English Text Society, 1888, Extra Series, 52.

BURCHARD OF MOUNT ZION. *Descriptio Terrae Sanctae*, in J. C. Laurent, *Peregrinatores Medii Aevi Quatuor*, Leipzig, 1864. Translated by A. Stewart for the Palestine Pilgrims' Text Society, 1896.

BURTON, ROBERT. *The Anatomy of Melancholy*, ed. by A. R. Shilleto, 3 vols. 1893. For lists of Burton's books as distributed between The Bodleian Library and the Library of Christ Church, Oxford, see Oxford Bibliographical Society. 'Proceedings and Papers,' vol. I, part III, 1925.

CAESARIUS OF HEISTERBACH, *Dialogus Miraculorum*, ed. by J. Strange, Cologne, 1851. Translated by H. von E. Scott and C. C. Swinton Bland in the Broadway Medieval Library, 1929.

CARPINI. *The Texts and Versions of John de Plano Carpini and W. de Rubruquis as printed by Hakluyt in* 1598, ed. with valuable notes by C. R. Beazley (Hakluyt Society), 1903. Hakluyt's version is also printed in A. W. Pollard's edition of Mandeville. See under Pollard.

CHALMERS, ALEX. *The General Bibliographical Dictionary* (article on Mandeville).

CLAVIJO. *Embassy to Tamerlane*, 1403–6. Translated by Guy le Strange (Broadway Travellers), 1928.

CORDIER, H. *Mélanges d'Histoire et de Géographie Orientales*, Paris, 1914, vol. I (contains a Mandeville bibliography). See under Odoric.

CRAMER, N. A. *De Reis van Jan van Mandeville* Leiden, 1908. (Dutch text, with notes).

CRONE, G. R. *The Hereford World Map*, 1948.

DAVIES, H. W. *Bernhard von Breydenbach and his journey to the Holy Land*, 1483–4, 1911.

DRUCE, G. C. An account . . . of the Ant-lion,' in *Antiquaries Journal*, October, 1923.

ECCARD, J. G. *De Origine Germanorum*, 1750.

EUGESIPPUS. *Tractatus de distanciis locorum Terrae Sanctae*, in Migne's *Patrologia Graeca*, CXXXIII, col. 991.

ESTIENNE, H. *A World of Wonders*, translated by R. C[arew], 1607.

GESSNER, C. F. *A.b.c. Buch, oder Grundliche Anweisung in welcher der zarten Jugend . . . in der Teutsch, Lateinische . . . den meisten Orientalisch Sprachen . . . ein leichter Weg gezeiget wird*. Leipzig, 1743.

Golden Legend, The. Lives of the Saints as Englished by William Caxton, Temple Classics Series, seven vols.

GÖRRES, J. J. *Die Teutschen Volksbücher*, 1807.

GREENWOOD, ALICE D. 'The Beginnings of English Prose' in vol. II of *Cambridge History of English Literature*. Contains a delightful study of Mandeville.

GREGORY OF TOURS. *Libri Miraculorum*, in Migne, *Patrologia Latina*, vol. LXXI.

GUILLEMARD, F. H. H. *Cruise of the Marchesa*, 1886.

HALLIWELL, J. O. *The Voiage and Travaile of Sir John Maundeville, Kt.*, 1839 (a reprint of the 1725 edition of the Cotton text).

ISIDORE OF SEVILLE. *Etymologiarum sive Originum*, ed. by W. M. Lindsay, Oxford, 1911.

JACKSON, I.'Who was Sir John Mandeville ?' in *Modern Language Review*. XXIII (1928), p. 466.

JACQUES DE VITRY. *Jacobi de Vitriaco . . . libri duo*, in Bongars, *Gesta Dei per Francos*, Hanover, 1611, vol. I, p. 1047.

JOHN OF WÜRZBURG. *Descriptio Terrae Sanctae* in Tobler, *Descriptiones Terrae Sanctae*, Leipzig, 1874, p. 108. Translated by A. Stewart in Palestine Pilgrims' Text Society, 1890.

HAITON (Hetoum). *La Flor de estoires de la terre d'Orient*, in *Recueil des historiens des Croisades*, Documents Arméniens, vol. II, 1906. (Latin and French versions are given. My references are to the Latin).

HAMELIUS, P. *Mandeville's Travels*, edited by P. Hamelius (the Cotton Version), Text, 1919: Introduction and Notes, 1923. Early English Text Society. Original Series, 153 and 154.

HARFF, ARNOLD VON. *The Pilgrimage of Arnold von Harff, Knight*, translated and edited by Malcolm Letts, 1946 (Hakluyt Society).

HESE, JOHN DE *Itinerarius* in Zarncke *Der Priester Johannes*, II, p. 159. See under Zarncke, F.

LETTS, MALCOLM. 'Prester John. Sources and Illustrations' in 'Notes and Queries,' 1945, vol. CLXXXVIII, pp. 178, 204, 246, 266; vol. CLXXXIX, p. 4. 'Prester John, a fourteenth cent. manuscript at Cambridge.' *Transactions* of the Royal Historical Society, fourth Series, vol. XXIX (1947), p. 19.

——. 'Sir John Mandeville.' 'Notes and Queries,' vol. CXCI, pp. 202, 275 vol. CXCII, pp. 46, 134, 224, 300, 494 vol. CXCIII, pp. 52, 200. Vol. CXCI, p. 7 (The Dry Tree); p. 47 (The Liver Sea); p. 140 (The Ark on Mount Ararat).

LOWES, J. L. 'The Dry Sea and the Carrenare' in *Modern Philology*, III (1905), p. 15.

LUDOLPH OF SUDHEIM OR SUHEIM. *De itinere Terrae Sanctae liber*, edited by F. Deycks. Stuttgart Litt. Verein, 1851, No. 25. Translated by A. Stewart in Palestine Pilgrims' Text Society, 1895.

MANDEVILLE, SIR JOHN. See under Ashton, Bovenschen, Cramer, Greenwood, Halliwell, Jackson, Hamelius, Letts, Nicholson, Oxford U.P., Pollard, Steiner, Stokes, Vogels, Yule.

MARIGNOLLI, JOHN DE. *Recollections of Eastern Travel* (1338–53), in Yule's *Cathay*, second ed., vol. III.

MAURUS, HRABANUS. *De Inventione Linguarum*, in Migne, *Patrologia Latina*, 107–112.

MICHEL, L. *Les Légendes épiques Carolingiennes dans l'oeuvre de Jean Outremeuse*, Liége, 1935.

MÜNSTER, SEBASTIAN. *Cosmographia*. Basel, 1545. For other editions see V. Hantzsch, *Seb. Münster, Leben, Werk, Wissenschaftliche Bedeutung*, Leipzig, 1898.

MURRAY, D. *The Black Book of Paisley*, 1885.

——. *John de Burdaeus or John de Burgundia, otherwise Sir John Mandeville and the Pestilence*, 1891.

MURRAY, HUGH. *Historical Account of Discoveries and Travels*, 1820.

NICHOLSON, E. W. B. Letters in 'The Academy,' 11 November, 1876; 12 February, 1881; 12 April, 1884. Article on Mandeville in *Encyclopedia Britannica* (with Yule).

ODORIC OF PORDENONE (1316–30). 'Travels' in Yule, *Cathay*, vol. II. Edited by H. Cordier in *Rec. de Voyages et de documents pour servir a l'histoire de la Géographie*, 1891.

——. *Liber de Terra Sancta*, in J. C. Laurent, *Peregrinatores Medii Aevi Quatuor*, Leipzig, 1864 (attributed to, but probably not by Odoric).

OUTREMEUSE, JEAN DE. *Ly Myreur des Histors*, edited by A. Borgnet and S. Bormans, six vols. Brussels, 1864–87. See under Michel.

OXFORD UNIVERSITY PRESS. The Voiage and Travaile of Syr John Mandeville, Knight, 1932. A reprint of East's text.

PARROT, J. J. F. W. VON, *Journey to Ararat*. Translated by W. D. Cooley (vol. I of Cooley, *The World Surveyed*), 1845.

POLLARD, A. W. *The Travels of Sir John Mandeville* (Cotton version modernised). Macmillan's Library of English Classics, 1900 (with Carpini, Rubruquis and Odoric).

POLO, MARCO. *The Book of Ser Marco Polo*, edited by Sir Henry Yule, two vols., third edition (reprinted) 1921.

POWER, EILEEN. 'The Opening of the Land Routes to Cathay,' in *Travel and Travellers of the Middle Ages*, ed. by A. P. Newton, 1926.

PRESTER, JOHN, see under Letts, Ross and Zarncke.

PURCHAS, S. *Hakluytus Posthumus, or Purchas his Pilgrimes*, Reprint, twenty vols. 1905.

RAY, JOHN. *Travels*, 9th edition. 1727.

RICOLD OF MONTE CROCE, in J. C. Laurent, *Peregrinatores Medii Aevi Quatuor*, Leipzig, 1864.

RIVO, RADULPHUS DE. *Gesta Pontificum Leodiensium*, in Chapeavillus, *Qui gesta pontificum Leodiensium scripserunt auctores praecipui*, Liége, 1612–16. Vol. III, p. 17.

RÖHRICHT, R. *Bibliotheca Geographica Palaestinae*, Berlin, 1890.

——. *Deutsche Pilgerreisen nach dem Heiligen Lande*, Innsbruck, 1900.

ROSS, E. DENISON. 'Prester John and the Empire of Ethiopia,' in *Travel and Travellers of the Middle Ages*, edited by A. P. Newton, 1926.

RUBRUQUIS, WILLIAM DE. *The Journeys of William de Rubruquis and John de Plano Carpini*, translated and edited by W. W. Rockhill, 1900. (Hakluyt Society). See also under Pollard.

SAEWULF. *Relatione de Peregrinatione Saewulfi ad Hierosolymam et Terram Sanctam*, in *Recueil des Voyages et de Mémoires*, Paris, 1839, IV, p. 833. Translated by Brownlow in Palestine Pilgrims' Text Society, 1892.

SISAM, K. *Fourteenth Century Verse and Prose*, 1921.

SCHRAMM, A. *Der Bilderschmuck der Frühdrucke*, vol. XXI.

STEINER, A. 'The date of Composition of Mandeville's Travels.' *Speculum*, IX (1934), p. 144.

STOKES, WHITLEY, in *Zeitschrift für Celtische Philologie*, 1899, II, pp. 1–63 228–312 (Irish text and translation of Mandeville's 'Travels.')

SYMON SIMEONIS. *Itineraria*, edited by James Nasmith, Cambridge, 1778. See articles by Mario Esposito in *Geog. Journal*, Nov. 1917; February, 1918.

TAYLOR, ISAAC. *The Alphabet*, 2 vols. 1883.

THEODORIC. *Theodoricus de Locis Sanctis*, edited by T. Tobler, St. Gallen, 1851. Translated by A. Stewart for Palestine Pilgrims' Text Society, 1891.

THIETMAR. *Iter ad Terram Sanctam*, ed. by T. Tobler, St. Gallen, 1851.

TORQUEMADA, ANTONIO DE. *The Spanish Mandeville of Miracles*, translated into English [by F. Walker], 1600.

VINCENT OF BEAUVAIS. *Specula*, 4 vols. Douai, 1624.

VOGELS, J. *Das Verhältniss der italienischen Version der Reisebeschreibung Mandeville's zur französischen*, in *Festschrift dem Gymnasium zu Mörs . . . gewidmet*, Bonn, 1882. Copy in the Bodleian Library. Not in the B.M.

——, *Die ungedruckten Lateinischen Versionen Mandeville's*, Crefeld, 1886.

——, *Handschriftliche Untersuchungen über die englische Version Mandeville's*, in *Jahresbericht über das Realgymnasium zu Crefeld*, Crefeld, 1890.

WARNER, G. F. *The Buke of John Mandevill*, edited for the Roxburghe Club (Egerton version), with a French text, Harley 4383, supplemented by Sloane 1464, Royal 20, Bx. II, and Grenville XXXIX (now Add. 33,757). Reproductions of twenty-eight miniatures from Add. MS. 24,189.

——, Article on Mandeville in *Dictionary of National Biography*.

WILLIAM OF TRIPOLI. *Tractatus de Statu Saracenorum*, in Prutz *Kulturgeschichte der Kreuzzüge*, 1883, p. 575.

YULE, SIR H. *Cathay and the Way Thither*, second edition, 4 vols., 1915–16 (Hakluyt Society). Article on Mandeville in *Encyclopedia Britannica* (with Nicholson).

ZANTFLIET, C. *Chronicle*, in Martène and Durand, *Veterum Scriptorum et Monumentorum amplissima collectio*, Paris, 1724–29. Vol. V, p. 299.

ZARNCKE, F. 'Der Priester Johannes' in *Abhandlungen der phil. hist. Classe der K. Sächsischen Gesellschaft d. Wissenschaften*, No. VII (1879), No. VIII (1883).

INDEX

A

Abbey of Monks at Cassay, 64, 130
Abraham, the Patriarch, 47, 104, 130
Acre, capture of, 50, 141
Adam and Eve, their cave at Hebron, 47
Adamant rocks, 40, 57, 78, 84
Aden, 79
Adrianople, 145
Agrippaige, 139
Aix, Albert of, 32, 145
Aix-la-Chapelle, 148
Alexander the Great, 29, 61, 68, 74, 80, 104, 111; his correspondence with the Brahman king, 96; his visit to the Trees of the Sun and the Moon, 97, 117, 140; uses pigs against elephants, 142, 143; his columns, 142
Alexandria, Mandeville a *bailli* there, 108; water-supply of, 41
Alphabets, Ch. XVII; p. 53
Amazons, the, 31, 53, 136; queen of, and Gog and Magog, 74
Anselm, Friar, 48
Anthropophagi, 62
Anti-Christ, 74
Antipodes, theory of, 27, 40
Ants, gold-digging, 98, 105
Apples, Adam's, 44; of Paradise, 44
Apples as food, 96, 103
Ararat, Mt. Ark on, 31, 53, 104, 136
Arculf, a pilgrim, 48
Ark on Mt. Ararat, 31, 53, 104, 136
Arka, river, 49
Armenia, Little, 53
Ashton, John, his edition of the 'Travels,' 9, 121, 122
Assassins, *see* Old Man of the Mountain
Astley's Voyages, 35
Astomi, dwarfs, 96
Astrolabe, Mandeville's use of, 28
Astrologers at the Court of the Great Chan, 68, 70
Athos, Mt., windless summit of, 43
Avalon, 108, 141
Avatcha, River, 62
Avignon, 24, 162

B

Babel, Tower of, 54, 77, 104

Bale, John, his account of Mandeville, 34
Balsam Garden, near Cairo, 45, 129, 134
Bamboos, giant, 61
Bardi, Florentine banking-house, 25
Basilisks, 95
Bastards, test for, 105
Baudinet, Ogier's bastard son, 118
Beaumare, river, 96
Becket's shrine, 34
Bedouins, 44, 47, 137
Behaim, Martin, 79
Bethlehem, 48
Bigon, a drink, 64
Black Death, 24, 61
Boars, monstrous, 96
Boldensele, William of, Mandeville's use of his book, 32, 42, 43, 45, 46, 47, 49, 50, 147
Bourgogne, J. de, *See under* Mandeville
Bovenschen, Dr. A., 10, 29, 123, 124
Brahmans, their island and dealings with Alexander the Great, 96, 110, 165
Breydenbach, Dean of Mainz, 46, 152, 158
Browne, Sir Thos., 36, 78
Bruges, merchants of, 136
Brussels, MS 10420, 111, 113ff; 147, 153, 155, 156, 157, 159; quoted 116ff.
Bullein, Wm. 39
Bunyan, J. His description of the Valley of the Shadow of Death, 89
Burchard of Mt. Sion, 32
Burton, Robert, 36

C

Caesar, Julius, quoted, 95
Caesarius of Heisterbach, 50
Cairo, balsam garden at, 45
Calahelic, Sultan, 16
Calamaye, see Mabaron
Calonak, King of, his elephants and progeny, 61, 142; miracle of the fish, 62, 139
Camaka, rich silk cloth, 60
Cambalech (Peking), 30, 65ff
Cannibals, 39, 75, 95, 104
Canterbury, 34
Canton, 64

A PICTURE MAP FOR MANDEVILLE'S TRAVELS